TOWARDS A FEMINIST CHRISTOLOGY

Towards a Feminist Christology

Jesus of Nazareth, European Women, and the Christological Crisis

JULIE M. HOPKINS

WILLIAM B. EERDMANS PUBLISHING COMPANY
GRAND RAPIDS, MICHIGAN

© 1994 Kok Pharos Publishing House
Kampen, the Netherlands

This edition published 1995 in the United States of America
through special arrangement with Kok Pharos by
Wm. B. Eerdmans Publishing Co.
255 Jefferson Ave. S.E., Grand Rapids, Michigan 49503

Printed in the United States of America

00 99 98 97 96 95   7 6 5 4 3 2 1

ISBN 0-8028-4074-4 (pbk.)

CONTENTS

ACKNOWLEDGEMENTS

This book is the fruit of a long and difficult journey beyond the landmarks of the christology I inherited from church and traditional theology. I have not made this journey alone, at every step I have encountered colleagues and friends who have sustained, encouraged and inspired me. I wish to thank those who with patience nurtured and stimulated me in the years of confused wandering which preceded the discovery of a new and healing path. In particular, Kathleen Court, Joy Blackaby, Elinor Kapp, Morris West, John Kent and the late Ken Rawnsley.

Since joining the 'European Society of Women in Theological Research' and moving to the Netherlands, the journey has taken on the form of a communal pilgrimage where struggle and celebration have enriched my life and spirituality. In particular I wish to thank my sister feminist theologians, Manuela Kalsky, Doris Strahm, Lene Sjørup, Marijna Hoogerwerf, Mary Grey, Elisabeth Schüssler Fiorenza, Rosemary Radford Ruether, Daphne Hampson and Mercy Amba Oduyoye who have in conversation deepened and enriched my christological reflection.

I am also grateful to my doctoral students past and present who challenged and sharpened my thinking, in particular, Anja van der Hart, Heleen Joziasse, Detlef Bohlken, Miryam van Veen, Sytze van der Laan, Hykina Booij and the German students who organised guest lectures on this book at the Humboldt University of Berlin. I hope that I have integrated their critical comments into the final version of this book.

Finally, I wish to thank those who have worked with me to produce this book. Manna Bronkhorst offered criticism and support at every stage of writing. Joy Blackaby proof read the text and Charlotte Methuen and Dirk van Keulen sorted out the technical computor details. My publisher, Kristin de Troyer has offered encouragement and good advice.

This book is dedicated to the memory of my father, Horatio Nelson Hopkins.

1

EUROPEAN WOMEN AND
THE CHRISTOLOGICAL CRISIS

'O woman, great is your faith!'[1]

This book is intended to stimulate debate concerning a Christian faith for our time and context. Christianity in Europe is facing unprecedented problems. The intellectual challenge of the Enlightenment and modernism in the Nineteenth Century has given way to a far more serious problem in the late Twentieth Century, namely the collapse of European religion as a cultural component of society. Whilst Enlightenment thinkers rejected the domination of morality and politics by the Church, modern Europeans simply do not consider Christianity relevant to ethics and society.

The reasons for this development are complex. Suffice it to say here that the appalling results of anti-semitism in Europe, the appeal of individualism and the socio-economic forces of secularisation are factors which since the Second World War have eroded the very possibility of belonging to a church in the West. Christians are now the exception rather than the rule, they feel their identity to be under threat and have a tendency either to keep their religion behind closed church doors or become aggressively fundamentalist. Since the late 1950's with the arrival of Muslim, Hindu, Sikh and Afro-Caribbean immigrants and guest-workers, white Western Christians have had to adapt to multi-racial, pluralistic religious societies which has further undermined their sense of being the guardians of universal religious truths and values. The collapse of socialism as an alternative ideology to social-democratic capitalism in the mid 1980's has only increased the sense of spiritual and social confusion. Christians are suffering from an identity crisis precisely when Europeans are faced with the outlook of a soul-less future expressed only in terms of market economic activity. In this sense European culture is facing an ideological and spiritual vacuum and the churches have no alternative vision to offer.

It is in this context of the breakdown in the European Christian consensus that feminist theology has emerged. Her critique of Christian theology and ecclesiastical structures was originally based upon the emancipatory ideas of the Enlightenment. In this sense she seemed to many Churchmen to be 'the enemy within'. However I would argue quite differently. Feminist theology is the last gasp of many thinking women in the churches to renew the faith before Christianity perishes for lack of vision. Emancipation in the sense of equal rights and responsibilities is only the first stage of the feminist theological vision. Her goal is the critical transformation of women and men into a new way of being church where salvation in its broadest sense as physical, social and spiritual fullness is enjoyed and shared as a sign of hope to the world[2].

Sadly many feminist Christian women have walked out of their churches in frustration and anger. Others remain out of loyalty, although many are deeply unhappy with the core symbolism of Christianity. These essays are offered to both groups of women and to secular feminists who know little about Christianity but who are seeking a dialogue with Christian feminists as part of their search for a way out of the European spiritual and cultural vacuum. I hope that women of faith inside and outside the churches will read them and find them a constructive help in the reshaping of christology which is so necessary at this juncture in western secularisation. In particular, I have written this book for women Protestant ministers who face the current christological crisis daily in their work and in their lives. I hope that it will encourage them not to give up the struggle, but to hold on and renew the faith without fear of criticism or despair.

The thoughts expressed in these essays are my personal response to the challenge posed by the feminist critique of traditional and contemporary christology. It is not an attempt to defend Christianity against these criticisms, I share them and have elsewhere offered my deconstruction of christology[3]. This book is therefore a second stage in the debate around the religious significance of Jesus of Nazareth for modern faith. The feminist critique has systematically exposed the layers of mystification and ideological abuse which has brought christology into disrepute in the eyes of many women. I have come to feel that this negative approach is finally emotionally and existentially unsatisfactory. Surely it must be possible to reconstruct a spiritually dynamic and intellectualy coherent Christianity based upon the core of stories and beliefs about Jesus which does not repeat the mistakes of the tradition?

Therefore while these essays do not provide an apologetic for classical christology, neither can they be described as post-christian. I am a Christian minister and theologian and as such I have been personally challenged by the discovery of how sexist christology is and how fundamental the changes must be if we are to reconstruct a Gospel which is good news for women and men. It is extremely difficult, once confronted by the negative aspects of Christianity, to move intellectually and existentially beyond critique to new ways forward. This is partly because the problem is so multi-faceted and complex. Christology is the corner-stone of systematic theology. If one pulls it out, or even shifts its position a little, soteriology, ecclesiology, pneumatology and ethics come tumbling down upon one's head.

A second problem facing any attempt to move beyond theological deconstruction to reconstruction is that one needs a certain consensus of belief. It is not the theologian's task to sit behind a wordprocessor and type up a new religion! Certainly if one accepts and works from a liberation theological perspective and method as I do, then theology is always the second step, a reflexion upon the praxis of daily life and faith of the oppressed, silenced or ignored believers. This reflexion should be communal; the faith- community or movement study, pray, critique and renew belief and praxis together. The work that I here offer therefore, is the fruit of a contextual Christian-feminist collective effort and as such it is the product of a process which has taken place over twenty years and is still going on.

The Case for Pluralistic and Contextual Christologies

This book is not an attempt to define the contours of a universally applicable christology. I do not think that this is possible or desirable. It is not possible because christology, as the theological reflexion upon the meaning of Jesus as the Saviour of Christians is not monolithic or uniform. Doris Strahm has demonstrated how the history of European christology can be considered as a series of discontinuous breaks rather than a continuous harmonious development[4]. This is not surprising

10

when we realise that tensions and differences in christology are already to be found in the New Testament writings. These, along with different cultural contexts and philosophical presuppositions led to debate and controversy throughout the first centuries of Christian missionary expansion. The Apostles', Athanasian, Nicean and Chalcedon creeds were not so much attempts at defining doctrine as doxological affirmations of faith within the general theological (and political) consensus of the day[5]. After that period of Early Catholicism the consensus broke down and the Church split into Latin Catholic and Eastern Orthodox. The rise of Protestantism in the Sixteenth Century is another example of a radical breakdown in doctrinal consensus.

Today the Western christological tradition is being challenged by vibrant new christologies emerging in Latin America, Africa, Asia and amongst the Black communities of the United States and Europe. These christologies are confessional, witnessing to the courage and faith of peoples whose lives were for centuries exploited by western colonial powers. Such christolgies, born out of suffering and resistance have little stake in the Greek dualistic categories or enlightenment rationalism of European philosophy. For example, Mercy Amba Oduyoye and Elizabeth Amoah from Ghana write that 'an African woman perceives and accepts Christ as a woman and as an African'[6]. In saying this they are making two claims: firstly that African women know Jesus intimately and that he shares daily in their struggle to find food for their children, healing for their sickness and strength to live and work for a new and just African future, free from western paternalistic interference and internal corruption and bloodshed. Jesus is the power of African Christian women, they call upon him as their brother, chief, sister, mother and ancestor to conquor evil and affirm a renewed African consciousness based upon African culture and the liberation of women and men from patriarchy[7]. Secondly, by saying that Jesus is an African woman, Oduyoye and Amoah are claiming the right of African women theologians to reflect upon these experiences and beliefs as a basis for christology.

If culture and socio-economic conditions have such a formative influence upon christology, then one must accept that all christologies are contextual and that this relativises our understanding of truth. Perhaps it is impossible to fully understand the religious experience of persons from a different sex, class, race or culture. When Chung Hyun

11

Kyung writes about the problem of 'han', that is the spiritual and physical feeling of 'resentment, indignation, sense of defeat, resignation and nothingness' which afflicts women factory workers and peasants in South Korea, she is not describing an experience which feminists in the west could reinterpret in terms of the loneliness, exhaustion and depression of European working mothers[8]. 'Han' is a fundamentally different psychological and existential condition. Chung seeks liberation from 'han' in the shamanistic female tradition which is a key element in her Korean women's christology. A depressed western woman will most likely turn either to her doctor for tranquillizers or to her therapist. Her christology is unlikely to include a faith in the power of Jesus to exorcise evil spirits or heal her pain. The pervasive effect of the empirical sciences and western rationalism has removed 'the supernatural' from her faith and experience.

This observation leads to a second reason why a universal dogmatic christology is not possible, namely that people from different cultural and socio-economic contexts have different existential needs and therefore different understandings of what salvation is and how it is to be realised or received. It is dangerous to overgeneralise but I tend to agree with the Peruvian liberation theologian Gustavo Gutiérrez that the existential difference between people in the so-called third world and westerners is fundamental. He writes, 'A good part of contemporary theology seems to have arisen from the challenge of the nonbeliever. The nonbeliever questions our religious world, and demands a purification and profound renewal...In Latin America, however, the challenge does not come first and foremost from the nonbeliever. It comes from the nonperson. It comes from the person whom the prevailing social order fails to recognize as a person- the poor, the exploited, the ones systematically and legally despoiled of their humanness, the ones who scarcely know that they are persons.'[9]

If a monolithic christology is not possible, is it not at least desirable, something to which we should strive to aim for? In earlier days Christianity declared that there is no salvation outside the Church. Christology was misused as an ideological legitimation for witch hunts, the Inquisition, colonial expansion, anti-semitism and religious wars. The anathema has been promulgated against theologians, scientists and social reformers in the name of Christ. Women and homosexuals are still restricted from full participation in Christian congregations and

12

church leadership on the basis of their 'otherness' to Jesus the Christ. I agree with Sharon Welch who argues that the demand for doctrinal conformity is a dangerous form of religious hubris and imperialism. She writes, 'In the Christian tradition I find a pathological obsession with security, an obsession that impels the denial of difference (thus concern with heresy and essences), an obsession that leads to a blinding Christian triumphalism'[10]. Dogmatic absolutism encourages the abuse of power because it denies the necessary openness for internal criticism and reform which a living faith requires. In this sense, I do not regard the desire for uniformity as a positive virtue.

If we are to avoid the absolutizing of our truth claims whilst striving for a vibrant religion and morality, we need to rediscover the original Protestant emphasis on faith as living without security, of living without evidence and proof in the love of God. Søren Kierkegaard has beautifully described such a faith as swimming above forty thousand fathoms of the sea of life. In this sense, the need for religious authority to legitimise our beliefs and actions can be viewed as a lack of faith in ourselves and our God. The Bible, the Creeds, confessions of faith, the sacraments, liturgies and hymn books are aids to faith, but only to the extent that they open the possibility to disclosures of the divine. They are mediums to truth but not truth itself. This observation accords with the post-modernist insight that our experience is to a great extent a social construction of language. The process of objectifying and ordering the world around us and developing a conscious ego is mediated to us through the language we learn as children. We need language to be human, to become self-conscious and to communicate and form relationships, but we are as much a text written by culture as we are subjects of our own thoughts. We cannot reach through to pure experience or reality beyond the language we have learned. All truth is then mediated, including religious truth[11]. We are then thrown back upon an old Christian insight, namely that all religious language is analogical or metaphorical and that some truth is best unsaid (the tradition of the via negativa).

The essays in this book are formal theological reflections upon aspects of christology. However, although the discourse may be rather theoretical, the intention is practical. The question I have posed to myself as I have written this book is, 'Can christology be approached in such a way that it becomes good news for modern European

13

women?' In other words, 'Is there a Gospel left to preach?' My answer to these questions is finally personal, and influenced by my confessional background as a British Baptist minister and feminist theologian working for the Gereformeerde Kerk in the Netherlands. These contexts have fundamentally affected the way I have experienced Jesus and the problems related to christology. To illustrate the personal and practical dimension lying behind these essays, I have attempted in the following pages to identify and analyse the specific problems with christology that I have encountered in the pastorate and in training theology students.

The Jesus of European Pietism and the Woman Protestant Minister

Since the Enlightenment and particularly since the Industrial Revolution in the Nineteenth Century, there have been cultural, political and economic forces at play which have sought to push the Church out of the public sphere and to confine her to the private sphere of the home, personal morality, individualistic piety and charity work. This is the same sphere where, according to the cultuaral stereotype, women and children belong. Secularisation, market economics, the modern form of capitalist democracy and a popular sentimentalising of Christianity have all here played a role.

This process of the domestication of Christianity has had an enormous effect upon the clergy. The reverend minister has lost much of his social status and with it his privileged political and economic influence in the local community. Once, browsing through the old records of my Baptist seminary in Bristol, I was amazed to read that one hundred years ago the male ordinands left their dirty shoes outside their doors every evening and that women servants cleaned them overnight! This no longer happens for, I would suggest, three reasons. Firstly women are no longer prepared to work as live-in servants. Secondly because of the impoverishment of the college such privileges have long since been waived as unnecessary luxuries. But thirdly, there has been a change of attitude; it is now considered good preparation for the Ministry for an ordinand to learn to do the most basic and humble daily chores for himself. The status of the minister has been

14

reversed. Whereas once he was considered to represent the ruling function of Christ the King to his congregation, now he is expected to personify the serving role of Jesus, washing the congregation's feet.

Rosemary Radford Ruether has called this shift in status and role, 'the feminisation of the clergy'[13]. One is confronted daily in the British media with the popular caricature of the emasculated minister, whether he be an Anglican priest or a Free Church pastor. He is a white-haired, absent-minded, kindly old gentleman whose main concerns are raising funds for his delapidated church buildings and 'not taking sides' in the political and social discussions of the day. He speaks in a high sing-song voice and cycles around on a dilapidated bicycle to drink tea and eat muffins with old ladies.

I would argue that it is within this context of a shift in cultural expectations and ecclesiastical power that women have gained access to the Protestant Ministry. Whilst there is evidence of radical women ministers amongst the Baptists and Quakers in the Seventeenth Century and the Methodists in the Eighteenth Century, these offices were soon closed to women as the new confessions became institutionalised. It is only recently, as the churches began to experience a loss of clergy man-power that women's calling to the Ministry was fully recognised. For how many men wish to be consigned to the foot-washing sphere?- and in any case, the demise of the influence of the Church has meant that congregations have become poorer, buildings are a constant problem and career prospects are diminished. In my opinion, if one looked carefully at the context behind the theological discussions concerning the access of women to the Ministry, one would find that practical considerations concerning money and manpower have almost always been the issues that have finally swayed the argument in favour of women.

Women ministers are generally called to work either in ecumenical teams or in small struggling congregations. It is therefore not in wealthy suburbia or picturesque country villages that they are to be found but in large, secular, multi-cultural cities beset with social problems and moral confusion. Amsterdam in the Netherlands is typical of such a context. Here there are only a small percentage of churches left, struggling to survive and keep their confessional identity. There are over 40 women Protestant ministers and Roman Catholic women pastoral workers employed here, mainly on a part-time basis.

They live often with young families, in small flats in the poorest parts of the city, and they are all overworked. They function, not only to hold together their small congregations through preaching, teaching, administration, fund-raising and pastoral support, but also to work as chaplains to the city hospitals, prisons, old people's homes, psychiatric institutions, factories and colleges. They organise projects and train and support volunteers working with drug addicts, AIDS patients, the homeless, refugees, battered women and alienated youth. These women are the serving hands and feet of Christ; they are personifications of the unconditional sacrificial love of Jesus.

However, these women began to perceive that an unbridled passion to love and care for everybody and redeem Amsterdam could prove a motor for self-destruction. Some have had nervous breakdowns, others are burnt out, depressed or sick or have lost their faith. In 1990 they came together to form a support and consciousness-raising group; they named their club 'Eve around Amsterdam'. Now they regularly organise study days for their own in-service training, to develop new theory and practice for the pastorate based upon a developing critical awareness of the dynamics of power in church and theology which pressurise women to offer themselves up as living sacrifices, to collude in their own exploitation and self-denial in the name of Christ. These women, and many other women ministers have begun to realise that there is something fundamentally wrong with the health of the Christian Ministry and that this is inextricably linked with gender relations and christological beliefs.

This complex of problems constitute a contemporary christological crisis for theologically trained women. In this essay I shall analyse this crisis only in relation to the practical experience of women Protestant ministers from the so-called Free Church tradition. However, elsewhere I have offered a formal theological critique of the main difficulties and many of my observations reappear later in this book. However, before I proceed, I should like to emphasise that many lay Christian women are also presently wrestling with the negative consequencies of inherited christological doctrine. How many it is impossible to calculate since these women do not have access to a public platform within the churches and in any case to openly question the teaching of the churches concerning Jesus Christ is in many congregations regarded as tauntamount to heresy.

I have conducted a pilot study with student ministers of the Dutch Gereformeerde Kerk into the beliefs and religious experiences of 'average' women churchgoers from thirty different congregations[14]. The results so far confirm my thesis that there is a christological crisis amongst Christian women. Only five of the thirty women interviewed believed that Jesus is divine, the Son of God or our redeemer. The rest offered images of Jesus as a prophet, a Jewish rabbi, a special person, an exemplar of equality between the sexes or a model of morality. Ten women said that Jesus played no role in their lives. Six women specifically denied that Christ is divine. Many women expressed resistance or even revulsion towards the classical atonement theory. A Church Secretary said emphatically, 'I cannot accept that Jesus has paid for my sins. Don't I have my own responsibilities? I do not believe that he would have found that good either. No, in that sense he does not play any role in my life, absolutely not!' I suspect this pattern to be widespead in our churches. Christian women who are the backbone of their congregations, who faithfully attend church services and give generously of their time, money and care, no longer believe the christological doctrines they hear weekly espoused from the pulpit or lyrically portrayed in their hymn books.

Something has happened. There has been a shift in christological beliefs amongst Christian women over the last 10-15 years, a shift that for many lay church women has happened gradually and unconsciously along with the development of a new sense of female subjectivity. However, for theologically trained women ministers, this process has become conscious and visible and it now poses a threat to their careers and their relationship to their congregations, for as preachers and pastors they are responsible for the apologetical handing on of the faith and Christian tradition. Women ministers then, embody the christological crisis and are the most vulnerable to charges of heresy, 'radical feminism' or 'post-modernism' because they are public examples of a more general reworking of beliefs amongst western Christian women.

In practical terms, based upon pastoral experience, how should I describe the causes of this crisis or shift in christology? My analysis is as follows. The western Protestant cultural stereotype of the Christian 'woman' is that she is a spiritually intuitive, caring mother who is prepared to sacrifice everything for the wellbeing of her children and husband. This image has co-incided since the Industrial

Revolution with a correlative pietistic stereotype of Jesus as the self-sacrificing child of God who proclaimed a personal conversion to a religion based upon an ethic of care, love of a fatherly God and moral discipline. In other words, the gentle Jesus who went as a lamb to the slaughter to save us from our sins and the ideal wife and mother are both cultural symbols for the same yearnings for security and unconditional love at a time of rapid and aggressive socioeconomic and technological change. These stereotypes have encouraged in evangelical, pietistic and pentecostal circles a certain idealisation of the 'feminine' and the so-called 'feminine virtues' of charity, care, gentleness, patience, humility, self-denial and sacrificial love. The effect of this sublimation of the 'feminine' has been to reinforce the attitude that religion is a private affair and to concentrate morality upon the individual within the family.

A stereotype is not a description of reality but an image created through a social consensus as to how reality is wished to be and how these wishes should be expressed through behaviour, values and relationships. Gender stereotypes are socialised into babies and children through the influence of parents, school, the media and dominant peer groups. Religious stereotypes are further reinforced by Sunday School, Church worship and Christian doctrine. My thesis is that in popular pietism, gender and christological stereotypes reinforce each other. A devout teenage girl who believes herself to be called to the Christian Ministry has to a lesser or greater degree imbibed the correlative stereotypes. Thus she may simultaneously feel an identification with the mission of Jesus and be in love with him. This can give her enormous resources of courage and inspiration. In the energy and idealism of youth she may fight every man-made barrier to her goal of ordination. With passion and commitment she will attempt to prove herself a perfect candidate, intellectually, morally and spiritually.

Problems arise however, once she is finally ordained and begins to work in the reality of the pastorate. For she is not a perfect stereotype either of the artificial feminine or of the sacrificial Jesus. She can attempt to embody these reinforcing stereotypes by selflessly serving her congregation and 'the needy', living out as it were, a public ideal persona. But sooner or later her rigorous perfectionism will prove too heavy a burden to bear. At this point, her work can become a play, she will perform it but her innerlife is plagued with a sense of guilt, failure and anxiety that her 'flock' should discover the awful truth. If a woman minister lacks the personal or communal resources necessary to break through the stereotypes she can become ill or suffer a nervous breakdown. If this does occur, it tends to reinforce the feminine stereotype because, 'as everybody knows' women are weaker than men physically and more prone to neurosis. If they attempt to exercise leadership they bring suffering upon themselves and their families.

The internalised stereotypes of the woman minister are shared by her congregation who often, quite unconsciously, project impossible expectations upon her. These projections are gender specific. The women members of her congregation also cannot live up to the feminine-Jesus stereotype. They too feel failures, burdened with guilt and secretly tired and depressed from the constant demands upon them to be carers. Once however that they have a woman minister, they can release part of their heavy load by projecting their perfectionism and guilt onto her. They will idolise her if she successfully embodies the feminine-Jesus stereotype on their behalf, but if she begins to show flaws they will ruthlessly criticise her, for she has betrayed their trust by publicly exposing the guilt and failures of them all.

The men in the congregation have a double and contradictory set of expectations of their woman minister. On the one hand she is to be public proof that they are progressive, emancipated, good men, gentle and saintly who like Jesus embody the feminine virtues. She is their proof because they have organised her election to their congregation and she depends upon their goodwill to be a successful pastor. However, they also expect her to restrict her leadership to the private sphere of religion. They, as men of the world, understand about money, management and policy-making and she (and by implication, Jesus) should not interfere. Holiness must be contained and protected.

From this generalised overview, I have tried to show that where the two stereotypes of femininity and the pietistic Jesus fuse, there is unconscious collusion between the female pastor and her congregation to identify her with the serving, loving Jesus who redeems through sacrificial suffering. In such a situation, open communication based upon honesty becomes impossible. Expressions of frustration, anger and depression are taboo. The scene is set for a farce that could easily develop into a tragedy because the romantic and sado-masochistic elements in the plot could lead to an apotheosis where the woman

19

minister offers herself up as a scapegoat for the relief of the communal failure and guilt. If in such a situation, the woman minister is to save herself from this fate, she will need to find the courage and strength to go through a painful process of self-examination. Finally she will need to let go of the feminine stereotype and the pietistic Jesus stereotype. However, once she begins upon this path of self liberation it is almost inevitable that she will also experience a crisis of faith, a christological crisis.

This crisis is both existential and theological. Protestantism is based upon a pessimistic view of human nature. Humanity is fallen through pride and egoism. With the Fall a curse was brought upon creation; suffering, corruption, evil and death are the inheritance of the children of Eve. Further, we deserve nothing less, it is a fit self inflicted punishment, as we continue to sin. In this sense we are paradoxically powerless to change our situation but also guiltily responsible for every form of misery[15]. Only the grace of God can save us, and this is mediated through the atoning death of Christ, for he is the Son of God and therefore the perfect redemptive sacrifice for our sin. It follows that salvation cannot be attained through human works; we must accept the unmerited grace of God without initiative or doubt. It is enough to remain humble and faithful, obeying the Word of God which is revealed in the Holy Scriptures.

If a Protestant woman wishes to define her own subjectivity, she cannot avoid challenging this doctrinal schema, for if the root of sin is pride, then any attempt at self-definition or self-assertion is sinful[16]. Once she rejects the Protestant definition of sin in order to emancipate herself from internalised stereotypes, she can develop a new understanding of love based upon a sense of self-worth and the balance between autonomy and relationality. Such a love, grounded in the loving nature of God, has no place for an atonement theory. As a German woman once said to me at a conference on christology, 'I may have done some wrong things in my life but I cannot imagine that what I have done and who I am could ever be so bad that God should require that someone should hang on a cross and die in agony to justify my existence'.[17]

It may well be that the concepts of sin and redemptive suffering should still have a place in our theology. These are fundamental aspects of human life. However it is clear from the above comment that some women have begun to take responsibility for their own decisions, action and lives and that it is within this changing context, where women are claiming the right to define their own subjectivity that the issue of christology should be addressed. It can no longer be assumed that the traditional Protestant schema of salvation answers to the longings for liberation and wholeness of contemporary European women; on the contrary, it may, as in the case of some woman Protestant ministers, hinder her work and block her energy.

Stereotypes can be changed. However the social pressures to conform are extremely pervasive and powerful. A woman Protestant minister who begins to let go of her double internalised inheritance is faced with emotional, practical and theological difficulties. She has to try and change her relationship with her congregation, and to develop a new christology which is truly liberating for women and men whilst retaining the support of her 'flock' who wish her to conform and protect their faith and identity at a time of rapid secularisation. I hope that these essays will encourage her to persevere and not to blame herself for having questions and doubts. I hope above all, that this book will alleviate her sense of loneliness and strengthen her sense of faith in herself and the God in whom she lives and moves and has her being.

2

JESUS: OBJECT OF RESEARCH
AND FOCUS OF FAITH

'Woman believe me, the hour is coming'[1]

Are faith and reason compatible? I should choose to answer, 'yes'. My answer is based upon how I interpret the biblical witness to the nature and actions of God and upon my own religious experience. In both cases God is revealed as the Source, Ground and Life Energy of all natural processes. Since I participate in nature as an organic being with rational and emotional faculties, I learn to know and love the Holy Ground of my embodied self as I try to think and feel with integrity. This is my theological presupposition, an act of faith indeed, but with very scientific consequences. For, if faith is open to critical reason, then christology should be based upon the historical sources concerning Jesus of Nazareth.

The method of historical biblical criticism has been sifting these sources for two hundred years and has produced a huge body of scholarship concerning the nature and meaning of the texts and the veracity of the events that they witness to. To ignore the results, as many fundamentalist and evangelical Christians do, is to mystify Christianity by asserting that it can only be believed in blind faith. It may be, as Van Harvey claims, 'that the content of faith can as well be mediated through a historically false story of a certain kind as through a true one, through myth as through history. But having said this the conditions of belief vary from age to age'[2]. In my opinion, in the secular societies of the West, people have lost the capacity of symbolic imagination. A myth is assumed to be something false, the opposite of a truth. People believe that they have the right to 'the facts' before they come to a judgement. However naive this is, it is less naive than the fundamentalist approach. For here, the mythological, metaphorical and symbolic language of the Bible is interpreted literally; mythology and history are hopelessly confused which alienates thinking

22

people and actually hinders the growth of a contemporary form of faith.

There is a sense in which the Church has been its own worst enemy in its public presentation of Jesus of Nazareth. On the one hand, theologians and biblical scholars have been so obssessed with objective historical reconstruction that they have appeared in the cause of science to be agnostic. On the other hand, preachers, evangelists and Church leaders have pretended they know nothing about this research and have spoon-fed their flocks with dreamy images of Jesus which belong to the romantic pietistic tradition of the early Nineteenth Century. Women have been excluded until recently from the scholarly so-called 'quest of the historical Jesus' and from influence in the Ministry, so perhaps it is women who can bring some commonsense and practical faith to bear upon the Jesus of history versus the Christ of faith debate. With her challenging 'feminist historical- critical method' Elisabeth Schüssler Fiorenza has already laid the foundation stones upon which others may build[3].

In this essay, I shall confine myself to the question, how is it possible to describe Jesus of Nazareth as an historical person and remain a feminist Christian? This question is not as simple as it may at first appear. For the historical Jesus was not a Christian but a Jew. Further, although some theologians such as Leonard Swidler and Elizabeth Moltmann-Wendel have claimed that Jesus championed women over against patriarchal First Century Judaism, the facts point to a much more complex situation[4]. For if Jesus expressed emancipatory sentiments, these views belong to Judaism not to Christianity; they spring from the spirituality and ethics of tendencies within the Jewish Torah and prophetic tradition. And sometimes Jesus was not particularly emancipated; to call his mother 'woman' showed a lack of respect which does not accord with the Fifth Commandment, 'Honour your father and your mother'[5]. I tend to agree with Judith Ochshorn who writes, 'Jesus was neither a feminist nor a misogynist. His central message simply lay elsewhere.'[6]

The question then is, who was Jesus and what was his message and is it possible or legitimate to appropriate that message today in a way that correlates with feminist political and spiritual aspirations? Daphne Hampson would probably add, and is it worth all the effort? In her public debate with Rosemary Radford Ruether, she argued, 'Feminist

23

women have had the courage to be their own authority. Is it not galling then, and in contradiction with feminist ways of acting, to admit to an authority which lies outside oneself; to agree that things will be determined with reference to the past, or determined by a church in which one has no real power and in which decisions (even decisions which primarily concern women) are taken by men?[7] Hampson's point is that to have faith in God and faith in oneself as a woman, it is not necessary to have faith in Jesus, a male revelation of God who lived two thousand years ago. This is a reasonable position considering the fact of religious pluralism. There is, in the phrase of John Hick, 'a plurality of saving human responses to the ultimate divine Reality'[8].

To have a relationship with a figure from two thousand years ago whose life is described in four short heavily edited texts does appear to many to be absurd. Further, for women there is an added problem. The main historical sources, the synoptic gospels, Matthew, Mark and Luke, were written by men who shared many of the patriarchal assumptions of the Greco-Roman world and therefore their accounts of Jesus are embedded in androcentric language and norms. Even if one is able, with the help of biblical criticism, to strip away the editorial influence and expose the earliest layers of the oral tradition concerning Jesus, one is still confronted as a woman believer with the fundamental problem of identification with a male messianic prophet. Schüssler Fiorenza has argued, 'A feminist theologian must question whether the historical man, Jesus of Nazareth, can be a role model for contemporary women, since feminist psychologists point out that liberation means the struggle of women to free themselves from all internalised male norms and models'[9].

It may be argued that these criticisms from feminist theologians are based upon a misconception, for Christians do not have a relationship with the historical Jesus but with the Christ of faith who transcends time and space and is Lord of all. In my opinion this is not an answer but a mystification. How can one possibly relate to an cosmic principle who is eternally being begotten, surrendered and then reunited within the Godhead? It is not simply that such a metaphysical concept is incomprehensible. My point is that such an abstract notion of Christ is totally irrelevant to modern Christian spirituality and social engagement. If the Christ of faith is not the Christian experience of the living presence of the Jesus of Nazareth whom we encounter through the earliest memories of the churches then Christianity is not rooted in human experience and cannot answer to human aspirations for salvation and liberation.

In practice, all Christians including theologians and biblical scholars consciously or unconsciously identify with the person and mission of Jesus of Nazareth. Their life-relation with him is the focus and medium of their faith in God. Through reflection upon the life, death and resurrection of Jesus in the cycle of the liturgical year, Christians make their pilgrimage through life. Identification is a powerful medium. Jesus is as it were a mirror to the inner world and daily life of his followers. This identification can become dangerous if it is denied. Those who unconsciously project their own image onto Jesus can abuse the gospels by using them as a legitimisation of their own ambitions to power. The historical-critical method is neccessary precisely to prevent such abuse. Once we have read the Dead Sea Scrolls or discussed with talmudic scholars the meaning of various sayings of Jesus we can no longer imagine him as a blond-haired blue-eyed Aryan.

The question therefore arises, what are the legitimate limits of projection? If as Ruether claims, 'One's portrait of Jesus ultimately expresses one's own normative statement about the Christian message to the world today'[10], how can we be sure our Jesus is not simply wishful thinking? This is a fundamental issue which has dogged theology for the last hundred years. In the Nineteenth Century, countless scholars attempted to write 'lives of Jesus'. In his famous book, 'The Quest of the Historical Jesus', Albert Schweitzer reviewed these attempts using historical criticism amd concluded that they were all based upon post-Enlightenment feelings and aspirations which had nothing to do with the ascetical world-denying Jesus[11]. Jesus was not to be confused with pietistic liberal philanthropy but rather he belonged to the Jewish doom-laden apocalyptic world of the First Century. This scepticism, further reinforced by the development of Form Criticism, led to the abandonment of the quest for fifty years.

A new generation of theologians led by Karl Barth, rejected the idea that the kerygma (the central proclamation of the earliest Christians) had anything to do with historical knowledge of Jesus of Nazareth. The new christology of Dialectical Theology centered upon Christ as the Word of God revealed in the Bible and particularly in the actions of

God at the crucifixion and resurrection of Jesus. This Christ speaks through the preaching and sacraments as the believer listens in humble faith and obedience to God. It follows that Christ cannot be reached using natural knowledge and science or indeed through religious institutions, value systems, political ideologies or even religious consciousness. Christ as Son of God, reveals the transcendent 'Wholly Other' God as father and judge of humanity by breaking through the horizontal line of secular history 'from above'. This in-breaking happened at one point in history, the incarnation, but it also occours to the faithful hearer of the Word as a crisis moment of judgement and grace[12]. To respond to Christ is the end of secular history for the believer. He or she no longer belongs to the profane world of sin, the flesh and the devil but enters into a sacred history beyond time and space. His or her true life and future is hidden in eternity with Christ the Son of God and redeemer of sinful humanity.

Dialectical Theology could not sustain its radical understanding of Christ as the end of secular history for various reasons after the Second World War. John Macquarrie observed that the early 1960's 'marks a kind of watershed in religious thought'[13]. A new optimism was emerging which re-emphasised the need for a social dimension to salvation. Macquarrie suggested that the shift was affected by four factors: the death of the leading dialectical theologians, the new spirit of ecumenicism fostered by the Second Vatican Council, the rise of the Hegel-Marx-Bloch line of neo-Marxism and the dramatic rise of nationalism, counter-cultural movements and alternative technologies amongst minorites, sub-cultures and oppressed groups[14]. I would however add a fifth factor, the new quest of the historical Jesus. This was officially launched with a book of the same name by James Robinson in 1959[15].

Robinson claimed that Ernst Käsemann had already laid the foundations for the quest in 1953 by arguing that the kerygma can only be legitimate if it has some continuity with the historical Jesus and that the New Testament sources were specifically written to preserve and encapsulate his person and message. In other words the new quest was based upon a new understanding of what the genre 'gospel' is. It is not a biographical history book, Hellenistic romance, tragedy, handbook of rhetoric (chria) or a collection of miracles attributed to a god or divinized man (an aretalogy) but is in fact an entirely new literary form

26

which emerged from the earliest Christian communities[16]. These churches gathered together oral traditions about Jesus and incorporated them into liturgical and catechetical texts which they used in their communal religious life. At a later stage these texts were assembled by an editor into a collection. In the second half of the 2n d century these collections received the name 'evangelion' (English 'gospels'), a term which upto then was used for early Christian missionary preaching[17]. In the New Testament canon we have four such gospels but there are many others. The discovery of the Gospel of Thomas in the Nineteenth Century and the many important writings such as the Gospel of Mary and Gospel of Phillip found at Nag Hammadi in 1946 witness to the extraordinary literary achievement of the earliest Christian communities[18].

Research into the gospel genre reqires a new methodological approach which can take into account the intention of the writer (redaction criticism), the nature of the faith community from where it was produced (sociological reconstruction based on the First Century Jewish and Hellenistic context), the linguistic nature of the text (form, source, genre and rhetorical criticism, narratology and structuralism), the theological content of the gospel (biblical theology) and the principles of interpreting the text in today's faith community (dialogical hermeneutics). In other words, the new quest has attempted to reassert its scientific and objective nature.

The Prophet of Divine Destabilisation

If one asks how is it possible that the quest of the historical Jesus was relaunched after fifty years of dogmatic neo-orthodox theology, the answer must have something to do with an existential shift in European (and American) intellectual Christianity. I would explain it by saying that the eschatological message of Jesus began to be properly understood. Albert Schweitzer had described the eschatological consciousness of Jesus as doomladen and apocalyptic. Dialectical theologians asserted that the eschatalogical moment was for the faithful believer the end of the profane world and rebirth into the totally other sphere of the New Age beyond history. For example, in his criticism of Oscar Cullmann's suggestion that early Christians shared the Jewish sense of being caught up in a trajectory of 'salvation-history' (Heilsgeschichte), Rudolf Bultmann insisted, 'According to early Christian thought, Christ is the end of history and of the (Jewish?- my comment) history of salvation'[19]. But the tide was turning. The work of the English exegete C.H.Dodd finally reached Germany after the Second World War. Cullmann described Dodd's 'realised eschatology' as of foundational significance. He claimed that it was 'the exact antithesis' of the old position established by Albert Schweitzer. If for Schweitzer the Kingdom of God was exclusively an imminent future entity, Dodd's study of the parables demonstrated that they were intended to proclaim that the Kingdom 'has already dawned in the ultimate sense with Jesus' activity'.[19]

Today we are used to the evangelical category of realised or better, proleptic eschatology, that is, the tension between NOW and NOT YET in the gospel accounts of Jesus' life and message. For whilst Jesus announced the imminent arrival of the future reign of God, his healings, exorcisms and parables were signs that this New Age was already present and effective in his work. This sense of the utopian future Promise breaking into the historical present reflects a basic tension in Hebrew prophecy which emphasises simultaneouly the political, socio-economic and religious conditions necessary for salvation, and the actions of God in history as creator, righteous sovereign and saviour. In other words, Jewish eschatological hope involved the expectation of a coming together of the secular and sacred spheres in a balance of peace and justice, the promise of Shalom.

In my opinion, Rosemary Ruether has captured the essence of these beliefs in her description of Hebrew prophetism as the dialectical tension between two models of history which were believed simultaneously. According to her, one model is linear; salvation- history is understood as the journey of the People of God towards the Promised Land of Shalom. The journey is not always smooth however because there are conflicts between traditionalists and innovators, the establishment and the disestablished and critical poor. God reveals Godself in judgement and liberation through the vision and power given to those prophetic-messianic movements who seek to transcend the limits of prejudice and oppression to build a better society based upon the Promise. According to Ruether however, eschatological hope began to fade after the Golden Age of prophecy. Jewish sentiments became increasingly pessimisstic under the yoke of the Hellenistic and Roman occupations of Israel. By the period of Jesus, many believed that the End of the Age was approaching, that God would destroy the world and create a new one where God would reign directly as King of Israel. This apocalyptic dimension to Jewish eschatology can also be seen in the message of Jesus when he spoke of the signs of the End and the coming on the clouds of 'one as of a son of man'[23].

The second model of history is cyclical. Ruether claims that it is the ancient Hebrew hope for the Year of the Jubilees which is central to understanding the eschatological consciousness of Jesus. This was a deeply-held vision that the society should return to the conditions of the Great Shabbat through an act of communal conversion, once every fifty years. At the Year of the Jubilees, according to Leviticus 25 vv8-12, all slaves should be liberated, debts remitted, the land and property justly redistributed and the land left fallow and the animals and workers allowed to rest in peace for one year. In other words, on a generational basis the conditions of Shalom should be established in Israel. At the beginning of his public ministry, Jesus announced in his home synagogue in Nazareth that this year, as described in Isaiah 61 v.1-2 had arrived[24].

It is possible to criticise Ruether's interpretation of Jesus' eschatology at several points. However, the main features are shared today by a wide range of theologians and biblical scholars concerned with the reconstruction of primitive Christianity. These characteristics are, firstly, that Jesus was a Jew and that we can only understand his preaching on the Kingdom of God if we study Jewish eschatological and apocalyptic teaching and expectations of the time; secondly that Jesus understood himself as a prophet of the Kingdom of God. By implication, it follows that Jesus did not regard himself as the Jewish Messiah, for according to Jewish apocalyptic expectations, if the Messiah should come before the End of the Age he would be a political figure, a Davidic king who would restore Israel and reign for a thousand years to prepare for the End after which God would reign directly. Thirdly, that Jesus interpreted the signs of the coming Kingdom holistically; salvation would include physical wholeness, social justice and ecological balance as well as the renewal of religion and morality. He proclaimed that the firstfruits of this salvation were already present in his ministry; in this sense he may be described as a messianic prophet or the Last Prophet. Fourthly, that Jesus had a sense of urgency; he believed that the Kingdom was imminent and that people should repent and prepare themselves. Lastly, the eschatological dimension of the gospels is the key not only to understanding the person and mission of Jesus but also to the renewal of Christianity in the present.

Within this general consensus however, there is a wide range of permutations. Latin American liberation theologians have focused upon the revolutionary praxis of Galilean messianic movements which flourished before the destruction of the Temple and Jerusalem by the Romans in 70 C.E.. Others, encouraged by Jewish research of this period have attempted to identify Jesus with a particular sociological 'type' of Galilean charismatic prophet such as Honi[25]. There are scholars who, excited by the discovery of the Dead Sea Scrolls, have examined the ascetical communal life-style of the Essenes and concluded that Jesus shared their disgust for the corrupt Temple cult in Jerusalem and identified himself with their Teacher of Righteousness or the Zadokite High Priest who was to come at the End of the Age. Oscar Cullmann and others have sought to identify Jesus with the mysterious Son of Man figure portrayed in Daniel and the inter-testamental apocalyptic writings such as IV Enoch[26].

There has also been speculation concerning the inflences of wider religious and philosophical movements upon Jesus and the Primitive Church. For example, the widespread Mystery Religions, Zoroastrian dualism coming from Persia, the Greek traditions of the Pythagoreans and Cynics, Roman Stoicism and the identification of the Torah with Plato's Logos in the teaching of the Jew Philo of Alexandria. One of the most interesting developments in recent years has been the discovery of letters from the Jewish community at Elephantine in Egypt. This community had its own Temple dedicated to Yahweh and the goddess Isis. This has led to a line of scholarship developed by James Robinson and Elisabeth Fiorenza which has examined the link between Hellenistic Jewish Wisdom mythology, where creation, revelation and justice are described as the work of a pre-existent female hypostasis of God, 'Hokmah' (or in Greek, 'Sophia') and the wisdom sayings of Jesus. Was Jesus a sophos, a Jewish Wisdom teacher who came to be identified by his followers as the final emissary of Wisdom or Wisdom Herself?[27].

Whether Jesus understood himself as Wisdom or the last messianic prophet or the new Teacher of Rightousness is impossible to conclusively determine. We cannot reach back to the historical conciousness of Jesus as he was in himself, we are forced to rely on the gospel editors who combined the perspectival 'memory impression' of Jesus' first followers with the beliefs of their own Christian communities (Van Harvey[28]). However, it is in my opinion important to know that these were the roles available to the first Christians. For all these roles had, at the time of Jesus, an eschatological dimension. The coming of Wisdom, the Son of Man or another redemptive figure was the sign that the End of the Age was imminent and the Kingdom of God was at hand. The fact that Jesus was publicly humiliated and crucified must have reinforced this feeling of imminence and once the Temple was destroyed the moment had surely arrived! It is only possible to understand the Gospels and the letters of Paul if this atmosphere is appreciated. It is this eschatological sense of living on the brink of a divine revolution which gives the New Testament its special dynamism and persuasive power.

But the End did not come and the spreading Christian churches found themselves the butt of Roman persecution. In a long and difficult period of readjustment over four centuries, Christian communities adapted in lesser or greater degrees to the dominant Roman ethos and finally under the Emperor Constantine, the mainstream Church became the official cult of the Empire. Jesus was given the title 'Pantocrator', Lord of the Universe and instituted as the Messiah of Christendom who would reign with the emperors until the imperial Millenneum had run its course.

The question then arises, how is it possible to live with the sense of eschatological tension between the present and the future which is so much a part of the life and teaching of Jesus of Nazareth? At the time of Jesus, there were those of his countrymen who could not bear the tension. It is highly likely that the Zealots who precipitated the Jewish revolt against the Romans believed that they could force the End of the Age through a holy war. In fact their actions led to the destruction of the Holy City and finally to the Diaspora. The early Christians continued to wait for some time for the Second Coming of Jesus as their vindicator and judge of the beast of Rome but finally they capitulated to the imperial cult and were pacified.

In my opinion, a christology rooted in the historical Jesus and his embodied message of the eschatological Kingdom of God is a fundamental challenge to the contemporary western churches. For to get the balance right between practical realism and prophetic utopianism requires a spirituality where action and contemplation go hand in hand. It requires much faith, creative imagination and moral courage to live in our secular world in the destabilising presence of God. The Church has always been tempted either to misuse religion to gain cultural and political power or to succumb to passivity and deny the revolutionary dynamic of its faith. But if Jesus is to be believed, the signs of the future Promise are already amongst us if we have ears to hear and eyes to see. Our task is to identify and interpret the signs and in faith to live as closely as possible within the presence of the future Reign of God. This future, as we have already seen, is based upon social justice as well as personal salvation. Ruether writes, 'Closeness to the Kingdom is a matter of concrete reality, not ideology or institutional privilege. It is a matter of discerning the realities of liberation that are actually taking place. This is why those who discern the Kingdom are prophets and not merely sociologists'[29].

I have tried to demonstrate that by reviewing the scholarly discussion concerning the historical Jesus, it is possible to reconstruct something of the original message of Jesus. With the knowledge that biblical criticism affords, it is possible to interpret the synoptic gospels on the basis of their original meaning. In other words, the historical- critical method can open to contemporary readers the horizon of the original faith of the gospel writers. In order to enter into an existential relationship with the Jesus to whom they witness we can bring our contemporary horizon of meaning to that of the text and engage in a dialogue. For women, the dialogue must necessarily have a critical dimension because the text is androcentric, that it, it was written by men whose literary style reflected the grammatical conventions of the day where maleness was considered to be normative for humanity. The language of the text is therefore actually gender inclusive; the generic terms 'men' and 'brothers' include women and sisters unless it is stated to the contrary[30]. However, we have seen that for Jesus and his earliest disciples, it was not maleness or femaleness which constituted the norm of their gospel, but the imminence of the Kingdom of God.

The question still remains, is it legitimate to appropriate today the

32

embodied message of Jesus of Nazareth for feminist political and spiritual aspirations? Clearly in the hermeneutical dialogue between the faith-community who read the gospels and the Jesus of the gospels, it is a fact that the Christian agenda changes with context and time. Feminism was not an issue in First Century Palestine but neither were nuclear weapons, capitalist economics or genetic engineering. However, Christians look for guidelines on these and many other contemporary issues in the sayings and actions of Jesus. I do not think this is necessarily self-delusion. Jesus had very clear ethical principles which can be applied to a wide range of religious and socio-economic problems. Further, his parables and prophetic actions speak to the fundamental human experiences of daily life in a remarkable way. I would argue that this is because the personal loving, creative God to whom Jesus witnessed remains the Power and Ground of our world.

However, leaving metaphysics to one side, I would argue that feminists in search of an activist-contemplative spirituality based upon daily realism and utopian vision could find the Jesus of the synoptic gospels more interesting than they have been led to believe by the churches. It would be worth while at least to go and read the historical sources before coming to a decision to scrap the western religious tradition and begin something new. In particular women who have developed the art of reading the gospels *as women*, often observe that the historical Jesus focused his mission upon the poor, the sick and social outcasts of his day. Women are still the poorest members of western countries. Single parent mothers, part-time working women, black, migrant, chronically sick and elderly women constitute the poorest and most neglected layer of our societies. Jesus announced that the first shall be last and the last first in the Kingdom of God. This, I believe was the messianic message which cost him his life.

3

THE JESUS MOVEMENT
AND THE KINGDOM OF GOD

'Whoever does the will of God is my brother,
and sister, and mother'[1]

Elisabeth Schüssler Fiorenza has described the life of Jesus with his followers as a socio-religious movement.[2] According to her reconstruction of Christian origins, Jesus as the prophet of Sophia-God initiated a renewal movement within Palestinian Judaism. This movement had sectarian features. Its male and female participants abandoned their work and their homes to form an a-familial or anti-familial community. In smaller groups or sometimes all together they travelled through the Galilean villages relying upon alms and hospitality from well-wishers. As itinerent exorcists, healers and teachers, the disciples witnessed to the holy presence of God amongst the common folk of Israel. Their simple communal life-style and table hospitality were the eschatological signs that in the prophet Jesus the New Age had come near at hand. It was foretold that at the End of the Age, Sophia, the creative wisdom and justice of God would return from her exile from the world and invite the poor, the sick and the outcasts to her table of plenty. Perhaps the disciples believed that Jesus was a prophet of Sophia-God, a 'sophos', or perhaps they believed that he was Sophia (particularly in Matthew's Gospel). Whatever they thought or hoped, one thing is clear according to Fiorenza, their beliefs took a prophetic and ethical form. They rejected the current patriarchal social structures and eschewed external religious and familial obligations and formed a new sort of extended family based upon the belief that they were brothers and sisters, a 'discipleship of equals'[3].

By interpreting the life and work of Jesus within the context of a Jewish eschatalogical renewal movement, much light is thrown upon our reading of the Gospels. Further, new exegetical tools can be brought to bear in the rather worn out debate over 'was Jesus a feminist?' If we concentrate our attention only upon the sayings and parables of Jesus we cannot honestly conclude that he addressed the socio-economic and politico-religious dimensions of patriarchy. As Nicola Slee has shown for example, of the main characters in the synoptic parables of Jesus, 211 are male and only 21 female (of whom 10 are bridesmaids![4]). However, once the focus is shifted to the life-style and praxis of the Jesus Movement a new vision of power between the sexes in the inbreaking Kingdom of God is revealed. Not only in this divine revolutionary context shall the first be last and the last first, but within the community of the New Age the rule of the father is to be abandoned. God alone may be obeyed as a father, the disciples as children of God are brothers and sisters endowed with the Spirit according to their faith and commitment. Patriarchal hierarchy is radically undermined and replaced with mutual service and community of possessions and obligations.

The question arises as to what precisely was the nature of this Jesus Movement. That it existed, I find extremely plausible. For although Fiorenza's reseach is handicapped by the fact that we do not have extra-biblical literary evidence of the life of Jesus and his disciples, we can find other examples for First Century Jewish sectarianism, for example the Essene, Hasidim and Zealot movements. Further, there are interesting parallels between the radical instructions Jesus gave to his disciples as he sent them out to preach in the villages and what Diogenes Laertius described as the life-style of itinerant Cynic -Stoic charismatic preachers[5]. Both groups are allowed a single tunic, sandals, a staff and by implication a girdle. According to Howard Kee, the only difference in eqipment was that the Cynic-Stoic wandering philosopher-preachers carried a begging bag whereas according to Mark 6 v.8 Jesus forbade his followers to carry a begging bag or money; rather they were to seek food and hospitality at one place in each village.[6]

According to The Acts of the Apostles, the disciples continued to share their possessions and eat communally in the earliest Jewish Christian congregations (Acts 3 v.43-47). It is impossible to make a clear distinction between the practice of the original movement and that of the early churches from which the gospel writers came. Clearly their own communal life-style influenced their accounts of the Palestinian movement. However, original memories must have been passed on orally. How else are we to explain the negative portrayals of Peter as

35

the cowardly denyer of Jesus, James and John as power-hungry zealots and Thomas the doubter? These gospel character sketches of well-known male apostles witness to the tensions within the original Jesus Movement. It may have had a utopian and messianic vision but in practice such a socially and religiously alienated group lived under enormous stress. This aspect of their communal life is convincingly portrayed in the film of 'Jesus Christ Superstar' by Webber and Rice.[7]

That the sect not only survived after the crucifixion of Jesus, but developed into a dynamic missionary movement, is inexplicable unless one accepts, as James Dunn has argued, that Jesus had an exceptional consciousness of the power and presence of the Spirit of God which he could mediate to others[8]. In other words that his message was experienced, believed and practised by the movement with a messianic fervour. Further, that his followers did not accept that his death had destroyed his message or the Spirit through which it was proclaimed. The End was still imminent and as inheritors of the first-fruits of the New Age, the movement had the power and authority to speak in his name and through the same prophetic Spirit of God.

This point of view will be shared by many evangelical Christians. However, in my opinion it is necessary to take this line of reasoning one step further. When we read a gospel, we are reading a book written for a church or group of churches who believed themselves to be living by the spirit of Jesus at the edge of a catastrophe. Within a few years the divine revolution would be initiated and they must bear witness to it by living a radically different sort of communal life from that which was taken for granted in the Greco-Roman world. For this stance Christians were persecuted and martyred. This then is the social and religious context of the synoptic Gospels. It follows that everything we read in the Gospels is addressed to the situation of these communities; it is not an historical account of Jesus and his followers in the biographical sense. When therefore we wish to interpret the gospel stories for our contemporary faith-communities we first need to realise that our congregations today do not have the eschatalogical sense of urgency of the gospel writers, nor do we share a radically different life-style based upon communalist and egalitarian principles (at least not in the richer western lands). This means that contemporary christology and ecclesiology is confronted with a credibility gap. It claims to be based upon the biblical gospels, but it patently is not.

I do not have an answer to this problem but I do think that in the discussion on the principles of interpreting the New Testament (hermeneutics) we should adopt four guidelines. Firstly that we always try to place our portrayal of the Jesus of the gospels in the social and religious context of the community from which the gospel came (the *Sitz im Leben*). Secondly that we analyse the social and religious context of our own faith-community to clarify our own presuppositions and beliefs. Thirdly, that if we wish to preach or write about the person or mission of Jesus of Nazareth we honestly attempt to create a dialogue between our own faith-community and that of the gospel writers. In this dialogue the religious and socio-ethical standpoints of both communities should be honestly described and brought into conversation with each other. Perhaps we can learn from each other but there are bound to be differences of opinion, we are dialoguing across two thousand years of history! Finally, we should at all costs avoid identifying our own opinions, morality or beliefs with 'gospel principles', unless we are prepared to form a Jesus Movement along the lines of the original!

The Markan Portrait of Jesus

In this essay I wish to explore the portrait of Jesus and the Jesus Movement in the Gospel according to Mark. In order to do this in accordance with the hermeneutical guidelines I have suggested, I shall try to place these portraits within the setting of the Christian community from whence they came. To describe the Markan context I rely upon the research of Howard Kee who is the first biblical scholar to systematically attempt to reconstruct the Markan Sitz im Leben[9]. He has approached this challenge by analysing Mark in terms of three interrelated modes: the literary mode (literary conventions and traditions of the gospel as a whole), the conceptual mode (the vocabulary, style, rhetoric and theology of the text) and the social mode (the reconstruction of the socio-cultural context using sociological and historical models). As we shall see, Kee's unique approach radically affects our way of reading and interpreting Mark.

The question arises at the outset, why have I chosen to focus (solely) upon the Markan images of Jesus and the Kingdom of God? My answer is a mixture of logical deduction, christological curiosity and emotional involvement. From a logical point of view it follows from my hermeneutical guidelines that if one is to attempt to dialogue with the faith-communities behind the gospels one must make a choice. Each gospel was written by a different community and with the specific needs and beliefs of that community in mind. The contexts of Matthew, Mark, Luke and John were so different that it is unhelpful to fuse their accounts together. Interpretation then becomes an artificial attempt from today to impose an abstract unity upon historical Christian communites of two thousand years ago.

A further step in my reasoning is that I assume that Mark as the earliest gospel, reflects the most authentic memories and traditions of the Jesus Movement. Kee dates the writing of the gospel during the first Jewish revolt of the Jews against the Romans, most probably before the fall of Jerusalem and the destruction of the Temple in 70.C.E.[10]. It is here interesting to note that since the Second Century the Gospel according to Matthew has been placed first in the New Testament canon. This evaluation gained theological and dogmatic weight in the Fourth Century when Augustine declared Mark to be a slave following in the footsteps of Matthew. It was not until the 1860s that H.J.Holtzmann finally demonstrated the priority of Mark[11]. The reticence in acknowledging the priority of Mark and Mark as the main source for Matthew and Luke is in my opinion, a reflection of the Church's discomfort with the Markan portrait of Jesus.

Here we arrive at the second reason for my choice of Mark, the Markan christology, or better expressed, the lack of a doctrinal approach to Jesus in the gospel of Mark. Of the four gospels, Mark offers the least theological interpretation of Jesus' person. Mark does not have a birth narrative or a doctrine of incarnation. Further, there is no doctrine or even a theory of atonement. Most surprisingly there are no accounts of resurrection appearances. The Markan gospel ends abruptly with the women disciples fleeing in terror from the empty tomb. Biblical scholars have applied much ingenuity to account for this, with speculations concerning a lost ending to the gospel.

In 1901 William Wrede demonstrated that there is secrecy motif in Mark[12]. The beliefs surrounding who Jesus was are shrouded in esoteric comments to the inner circle of disciples. In Mark the parables are literally riddles or enigmas which can only be understood by the

Jesus Movement (Mark 4 v.34). In other words, Mark wrote his gospel for his own community who understood themselves as the faithful, suffering followers of Jesus who were awaiting the New Age. This community understood the secret veiled in the gospel, namely that their crucified teacher Jesus was a suffering messiah, the Son of Man, who was vindicated by God through the resurrection which they as a movement had witnessed and continued to experience as a reality through the Spirit. Christology for the Markan community was not a question of formulating theological concepts, but a way of life based upon a radically new form of ethics and communal practice in preparation for the social and religious revolution which God would initiate. In this Kingdom of God evil would be defeated and their suffering would be vindicated because they were the faithful guardians of the future.

If we wish to read the gospel of Mark honestly, we must take the life-style and beliefs of this community seriously. We cannot simply choose a theme or contemporary belief and superimpose it on the text. Faithful interpretation requires a dialogue. Once we have examined the socio-historical context of the Markan community and grasped their religious and ethical standpoint we need to do the same for our own faith-community. Then we shall be in a position to exchange experiences of God and visions of a redeemed community over the thousands of years that separate us. It may well be that our standpoints do not converge, I do not agree with Hans-Georg Gadamer that the reading of historical texts requires that we merge our horizon of meaning wholly with that of the text[13]. The dialogue may also have a confrontational aspect. For example, given the terrible history of the European pogroms and the Holocaust, the Christian claim that Jesus was the Jewish Messiah must be seriously questioned. It is not for me self-evident that I should believe that Jesus was the Jewish Messiah. I am not a Jew and I do not await the intervention of the Messiah before the End of the Age. However, the Markan community was certainly from a Semitic background. According to Kee, Mark shares most in form with the historical narratives of Jewish apocalyptic literature, in particular the Book of Daniel which is quoted in every chapter[14].

In trying to account for my choice of Mark I earlier wrote of an emotional involvement. In the final analysis, one's portrait of Jesus is a personal choice in which temperament and feeling play an important role. The Markan account appeals to me affectively. It is the only gospel which I enjoy reading as literature. The reason for this is for a great part connected with the particular Markan language, style and form. In contrast to the polished Greek of Matthew and Luke, Mark is written in a simple, semitically influenced Koiné Greek. This Middle Eastern village lingua franca suggests that his community came from southern Syria[15]. The vocabulary may be simple but it is direct and vivid. The use of superlatives and double negatives gives a heightened sense of the dramatic whilst the frequent use of 'immediately' or 'and' to join sections increases the sense of energy and movement. One can read the first chapters of Mark as a continuous narrative where events, sayings, character sketches, places and crowds of villagers press in upon each other to form a multi-coloured tapestry of life. The people in this tapestry are agricultural labourers, fishermen, alienated groups from the lower social strata and in particular women and children. It is the peasant world of Galilee which Mark contrasts approvingly with the wealthy hellenized cities such as Jerusalem.

Into this hard-working, suffering and socially oppressed pastoral world steps Jesus, the son of Joseph the carpenter of Nazareth. We are told that he had been south to the wilderness where he was baptised by John the Baptist. Afterwards the Spirit drove him into the desert where he wrestled with Satan. When John was arrested, 'Jesus came into Galilee, preaching the gospel of God, and saying, 'The time is fulfilled, and the kingdom of God is at hand; repent, and believe in the gospel' (Mark 1 v.14-15). From this simple introduction we learn that Jesus is a prophet endowed with the Spirit of God, that his life is a constant battle with the demonic forces of evil and that he has a new message, the End of the Age is imminent. Jesus the charismatic prophet and ethical teacher has made his appearance. 'Immediately', according to Mark, he seeks out two fishermen, Simon and Andrew to join him. In their home town of Capernaum he enters the synagogue on the Sabbath and begins to teach, 'And they were astonished at his teaching, for he taught them as one who had authority, and not as the scribes' (Mark 1 v.22). And 'immediately' he is confronted with a possessed man whom he exorcises. By sundown of that first evening, Jesus is surrounded by crowds of sick and possessed, 'the whole city was gathered together about the door' (Mark 1 v.33). The momentum of Mark is breath- taking, the urgency apparent, the kingdom of God for Jesus and for the Markan community was at hand!

In the 1970s western European women protested against the presence of cruise missiles at American airforce bases such as Greenham Common in England and Woensdrecht in the Netherlands. They attempted to shock the West out of its apathy towards the prospect of nuclear war by leaving their homes, families and work to set up camp outside the perimeter fences of the bases. They were physically mishandled, arrested and imprisoned by the police and portrayed by the press as communists and anti-social elements. However they stubbornly remained until the last cruise missile has now been removed and the Iron Curtain broken down. Those years of total commitment and communalism in the face of impending doom are perhaps for western feminists the nearest we have come to experiencing the climate of the Jesus Movement. Many women still remain alert for the future, but this is not apparent in the churches. Christians generally in the West feel pessimistic in the face of growing secularisation while any sense of urgency or divine-social revolution has been diverted into the heavenly sphere beyond or outside of history.

Towards an Intra-Faith Dialogue with the Markan Community

The question then arises, how can contemporary faith-communites read Mark and find an existential connection? This book is intended to demonstrate that for the Christian-feminist community the connection cannot be through traditional christological dogmas. We are seeking a fresh dialogue with the Jesus Movement and its message of the in-breaking of the kingdom of God. But how does one begin? To read the Markan narrative afresh without the mediation of two thousand years of Christian doctrinal interpretation is to be confronted with the strangeness of the text. The Markan world of First Century Palestine with its Jewish ethos and Greco-Roman culture has at first sight nothing in common with late Twentieth Century secular, technological Western social democracies. My suggestion is that we accept the strangeness of the Markan cultural context as our starting point. The dialogue is an inter-cultural encounter, and as with all dialogues between different peoples, each side needs time and space to define its own agenda and tell its own story. Honest dialogue thus begins with genuine listening to the 'other'.

The 'other', in this instance, the Markan community, tells us that Jesus was a prophet possessed by the Spirit of God who performed exorcisms and healings and taught under the influence of the Spirit. Many modern westerners would find this incredible and attempt to offer a rational explanation. In this sense they are not open to a genuine encounter with the other culture: they have already made the presupposition that it is primitive and inferior. Perhaps the alienation of the western spirit from religious experience is so complete that we no longer dare to take the risk of trusting our God-given capacities to play and dream in the deeper dimensions of the self. Women theologians from other cultures certainly do not suffer from this incapacity to appreciate the world of visions and wonders. Women from cultures as diverse as Ghana, Korea and Japan have claimed that Jesus was an (archetypal) shaman[16].

The shaman or spirit-medium plays a central role in the life of pastoral peoples, the urbanised poor, and social minorities the world over. She or he (shamans are mainly women) performs the function of interpreter of dreams, healer of the sick, exorciser of the possessed and wise teacher of the community for those who do not have the social influence or wealth to consult the institutionalised religious priesthood[17]. Mark Chapter 1 can be compared to many accounts of the secret calling, initiation, possession and final public appearance of a shaman. Jesus goes to the Jordan to be baptised by the older prophet John the Baptist, who has foretold that one shall come who is mightier than he and who shall baptise with the Spirit of God. As Jesus comes up out of the river he has a vision of the Spirit descending upon him like a dove. He hears a heavenly voice affirming his special calling. The Spirit drives Jesus into the desert where he fasts and fights the temptations of Satan. Finally master of himself and conqueror of the evil spirits, he enters Galilee empowered by the Spirit.

The calling, initiation and empowering of other Jewish prophets such as Elijah, Elisha, Jeremiah, Isaiah, Ezekiel and Daniel follow similar patterns. In Jewish shamanism, the Spirit of God is understood as the revealer of the words and will of the one true God. In this sense a Jewish prophet, possessed by the Spirit was primarily an ethical teacher and pronouncer of divine promise and judgement. In Mark's gospel,

42

both dimensions of the divine initiative are close at hand and in Chapter 13 are vividly described in apocalyptic proportions. In this context the exorcising of evil spirits is a sign that the social and cosmic demonic powers which oppress the people are already being defeated, the power of the rule of God is already partially revealed.

In my opinion, we cannot begin a dialogue with the Markan community unless we make the first step of accepting their account that Jesus exercised shamanistic or charismatic-prophetic powers. For they believed themselves to have inherited these gifts of the Spirit and continued to prophesy, teach, heal and exorcise in the name of Jesus. Further, it is only if we understand and accept shamanism as a genuine religious and social phenomenon that we can appreciate the peculiarly Markan emphasis on prophetic suffering. The suffering of Jesus and his warnings to his followers that they would share his suffering in the future, is a central theme in the gospel of Mark particularly in Chapters 11-16. This has led some feminist theologians to speak of the Markan Jesus as 'the wounded healer'. For example, Rita Nakashima Brock writes, 'The image of Jesus as exorcist is someone who has experienced his own demons...The temptation stories point to the image of the wounded healer, to an image of one who by his own experience understands vulnerability and internalized oppression. In having recovered their own hearts, healers have some understanding of the suffering of others.'[18]

Brock claims that the Markan Jesus healed by allowing the therapeutic power he had received to flow out of him to another who yearned for it. Each healing in the gospel is initiated by someone who in need and through faith created a relationship with Jesus in which brokenheartedness and healing were shared. Healing brought wholeness to the afflicted but also openness to the suffering and need of liberation of others. So a community of wounded healers grew up around Jesus who shared what Brock has called, 'the life-giving flow of erotic power'[19].

The Jesus Movement is reproached by Mark for failing to understand the deeper social and cosmic dimensions of suffering. Freed from physical pain and boyed up by the freedom of their itinerant communal life-style, the disciples fail to take the wider structural oppression of their society seriously. When Jesus is arrested and handed over to the occupying Roman army for interrogation, mock trial and execution they desert him. Apocalyptic images of conflict and death, the cry of despair of Jesus on the cross, 'My God, my God why have you abandoned me?' and the women fleeing in terror from the empty grave create a sombre ending to the gospel.

The messianic secret according to Mark is that Jesus reinterpreted the different Jewish strands of eschatological hopes for an agent of God at the Last Days in terms of 'the Son of Man'. This title, which Jesus sometimes used of himself, sometimes of a future figure, is a collective noun. It can mean the one sent by God to initiate redemption or the community who are redeemed through this agent. According to hints throughout Mark, Jesus chose to reject royal victorious messianic titles such as the Son of David, Son of God and Lord because he foresaw the inevitability of suffering for himself and his disciples. The conflict with the evil powers which held the people in bondage would require self-discipline and trust in the Spirit of God; persecution and even martyrdom were probable. In other words, the Jesus movement had discovered that the price for a new vision and society was very high. Their very existence as a pacifistic, radically different socio-religious community threatened the vested patriarchal, military and religious powers. The Markan community suffered ostracization and persecution as they fasted, watched and prayed for the End and their final vindication by God.

The shadow of the cross was a reality for the Markan community. Their teacher had been publicly humiliated and cruelly executed as a treasonist and blasphemer. Probably Mark was written during the First Jewish Revolt when Palestine was in uproar and the Romans had laid seige to Jerusalem. These events created an apocalytic mood, and one cannot avoid the impression that the community of Mark had millennarian tendencies. In our dialogue with this community we may wish to hold our distance from such a doom-laden atmosphere. However, I hope that we can still retain a serious approach to the problem of suffering and evil. The gospel of Mark was written in the context of the reality of the multi-faceted dimensions of evil. Those facets of structural evil still pervade our world. The reality of suffering created by the unjust distribution of wealth, knowledge and power demands a realism and analysis just as serious and ethically directed as that of the Jesus Movement.

If the earliest Christian communities, living as they believed in the time between two epochs, survived and spread, then they must have possessed spiritual and emotional resources. Clearly their new form of life-style based upon equality between the sexes, an ethic of service and care for each other and community of goods and possessions provided a powerful social cement. It was also a life-style with a missionary appeal in the Roman Empire; in spite of ruthless persecution the Movement, grew attracting in particular slaves and women from all social strata.

The Movement was however primarily a religious one. The radical life-style was a sign of the future, a utopian symbol for redemption. The gospel of Jesus and his followers was that this God-initiated future had already broken proleptically into history. The Movement was the first fruits of a promise from God that evil would be conquered and love, peace and justice would prevail. The Markan community could believe this in spite of their sufferings because of the resurrection of Jesus and his continuing presence with them through the Spirit which they shared. How do we know this, for there are no resurrection appearances in Mark? Many commentators have argued that the end of Mark after Ch.16 v.8 has been lost. The verses 9-19 which describe an appearance to Mary Magdalene, to two men in the countryside, and to the eleven disciples at table, were probably written a few years after Mark. Howard Kee argues persuasively that the absence of resurrection appearances comports fully with the Markan messianic secret. He shows that there are three passages where Jesus predicted his death to his inner circle of disciples and two where he foretold that afterwards he would meet them in Galilee, but that they did not understand[20]. Kee writes, 'By his account of their flight in terror, Mark lets his readers know that the resurrection, in spite of the predictions, was not expected, nor did the disciples even understand what it involved until after it had taken place'[21]. In Kee's opinion the Markan community did not require written biographical support for their belief in the resurrection because they had an existential relationship with their risen Jesus. Faith was a question of insight not information.

We who do not live in historical proximity to Jesus are faced with the challenge of holding onto the promises encapsulated in the gospel without enjoying the benefit of first hand experiences of the resurrection. It may be that for certain Christians the encounter with Jesus through ecstatic-visionary means is still a reality. The problem for

45

many feminist Christians is that this approach, which is emphasised in many Pentecostal and evangelical-charismatic churches is linked with a strongly patriarchal christology and oppressively male dominating morality and church order. My concern here however, is with the dialogue between Christian feminists who eschew abstract and dogmatic formulations about the risen Christ, and the Markan community. Can we circumnavigate orthodox christology and encounter for ourselves the power of the Spirit in the Markan story of Jesus?

If we examine the answers to this problem by feminist theologians, it becomes apparent that there are different approaches. In her dissertation, 'The Redemption of God', Carter Heyward sought to redefine our understanding of God using relational terms. The Jesus of Mark's gospel functions for her as the critical image of right-relation. Jesus' life demonstrates how radical redemptive power, authority and relationships can be incarnated when love of neighbour and liberation of the oppressed are given centre stage. Heyward rejects the belief in a physical resurrection. She wrote, 'It seems to me most faithful--empowering--to acknowledge the death of Jesus as the final act of contempt against this lover of God and humanity; and to acknowledge the resurrection as an event not in Jesus's life but rather in the lives of his friends.'[22] For Heyward, the spirit of Jesus continues to live although he died 'an unnecessary, violent death'[23]. He lives in her and in all her sisters and brothers who struggle for right-relation and liberation. In the ever-widening interconnected circles of lovers, friends, colleagues and political movements in which she lives, the messianic dynamic of Jesus is incarnated as divine revolutionary love.

Rita Nakashima Brock, who interprets the Markan Jesus less as a heroic figure but more as a medium of the therapeutic power which flowed within the Jesus Movement, offers a buddhistic metaphor of his death and resurrection. For her, Jesus was the white-cap of a wave in the sea. He emerged from the sea of Cosmic Being and was finally reabsorbed but the erotic power to heal the brokenheartedness in the world continues to flow through Christa/Community. Brock does not equate Christa/Community with the Christian Church, rather, 'Vast as the ocean, that community stretches far into the unexplored territores of erotic power. It is alive in the daily actions of those who, in small acts and large ones, live with courage, with heart.'[24]

Elisabeth Schüssler Fiorenza typically interprets the end of Mark as evidence of the problems within the new community of equals. According to Mark 16 v.8 the women disciples fled from the empty tomb. The Markan community, jealous of the apostolic role of Mary Magdalene, did not credit her with passing on the message that Jesus was risen and gone before the men disciples into Galilee.[25] Although logically she must have faithfully fulfilled her commission, otherwise the Markan community would not have existed! However Fiorenza concludes that the Markan community struggles to avoid the pattern of dominance and submission that characterizes its socio-cultural environment. Those who are the farthest from the centre of religious and political power, the slaves, the children, the gentiles, the women, become the paradigms of true discipleship.'[26] For Fiorenza, this community is connected with the religious and political struggle of feminists and female identified men today through its efforts to be the ekklesia of women. The historical continuity between the two movements is empirical and existential. Both movements are situated in the same patriarchal structures inherited from Aristotelian philosophy and Roman Law and both share the memories of the suffering and powerful foremothers of biblical religion. The resurrection is the revolt of all who have been denied their God-given right to participate in holy life.

These different feminist theological approaches to Markan christology and ecclesiology are at first glance extraordinary. Where have the women found the audacity to reinterpret the gospel so fundamentally? In my opinion, they have won the right to re-describe Mark because they have seriously listened to the Markan community with their own ears and out of their own (ignored) religious and social experience. For every motif in the work of these female exegetes is to be found in Mark if Christian doctrinal presuppositions are placed to one side. Christology both as a relational or erotic power, a messianic social and cosmic struggle against evil, a collective utopian experiment in faith and praxis and as a mystical secret discipleship of the Spirit-Sophia-God are all present in Mark's gospel for those with ears to hear.

4

THE CROSS OF POWERLESSNESS

'Woman, Behold your son!'

The evangelical slogan, 'the power of the cross to save sinners' is associated in the minds of many with a particular stereotype of preaching. The 'big' preacher (to use a Welsh expression), climbs to the podium or pulpit to the accompaniment of a 'moving' choir. His rhetoric can either take the soft 'I understand your problems and burdens' approach or the more theatrical hell-fire approach but the message is the same, we sinners crucifed Jesus. The sermon reaches a climax with the 'good news' that we do not need to feel guilty, we are not eternally damned after all because although we are personally responsible for the death of the Son of God and in fact deserve to be crucified ourselves, God has a plan to save us. He has accepted the death of Jesus in our place, his blood has paid the price for our sins.

This simple message of transactional guilt is extremely effective. As a suggestible teenager, only too aware of my failures towards my family, my church and my neighbours, the preaching of Billy Graham at the Albert Hall impressed me deeply. In that atmosphere, my feelings of guilt, inadequacy and insecurity were heightened to such a pitch that I felt I could see Jesus bloody and dying hanging on the cross in my place. It was a moment of tremendous relief and grace when I was told that this was the proof that God loved me. I was instantly 'converted' and came forward with many hundreds of others as an act of public witness.

It is often assumed that the emphasis upon a blood satisfaction for sin is a product of Victorian and German Protestant pietism. This is an over-simplification. The shedding or sprinkling of blood as a means of attaining salvific merit can be traced back to a complex of Jewish motifs that provided the religious background to Early Christianity. These motifs include Abraham's attempt to sacrifice his son Isaac, the Mosaic covenental bond at Mount Sinai, the slaughtering of the

Passover lambs, the sin-offerings in the Temple sacrificial cultus and in particular, the offering of the scapegoat for the sins of Israel by the High Priest on Yom Kippur (the Day of Atonement). This sacrificial background provided one strand in the New Testament attempts to explain the saving function of the cross. For example, the First Letter of Peter, which was written to Christians suffering persecution in Asia Minor, continually stresses the merit of unjustified suffering as a means of following Jesus who, 'bore our sins in his body on the tree that we might die to sin and live to righteousness'[1]. Christian servants and slaves are exorted to submit themselves patiently and with respect to brutal masters and women are required to be submissive to pagan husbands on the basis of this teaching[2].

However, the full Latin doctrine of atonement is attributed to the medieval theologian, Anselm of Canterbury[3]. The doctrine is based upon an analogy with the legally binding feudal relationship between a serf and his overlord. If a vassal subject contravened his obligations to his master or king, he was guilty of dishonouring his lord's justice and must make an offering or payment as satisfaction. Anselm argued that human sinfulness required penal punishment to satisfy the justice of God and that Jesus as the sinless Son of God paid the penalty with his own blood as the representative of humanity[4].

In her study of Christian redemption, the feminist theologian Mary Grey has argued that the emergence of Anselm's doctrine was the answer to a particular problem in the Western form of spirituality, namely guilt and the desire for grace in the face of the freedom and transcendence of God[5]. Medieval westerners had inherited the Roman sense of political and judicial life which stressed the passion of the gods for justice, that is the good ordering of nature and society. This is an interesting thesis which could be extended to explain the problem of guilt in our modern secular democratic societies. Is guilt, that sense of failing one's own values and norms, an existential condition of alienated human beings or is it an unnecessary and destructive product of Western forms of upbringing and socialisation? Even the Enlightenment concept of the autonomous free subject with responsibilities, duties and rights can be as burdensome for the Superego as old-fashioned Christian morality. Both ethics assume we personally know with our reason what is right and good so that if through passion or will we do what is wrong and bad we are debtors to our own integrity, society, the natural order of creation and/or God. Only punishemnt through suffering will redress the balance so that if we are not punished by others we punish ourselves. The sense of guilt as a product of a war between reason and body is a Western obsession.

Christian Masochism and the Existential Guilt of Women

In my opinion, the fact that guilt is an inheritance of Latin moral dualism does not justify a penal and substitionary doctrine of atonement. It is morally abhorrent to claim that God the Father demanded the self-sacrifice of his only Son to balance the scales of justice. A god who punishes through pain, despair and violent death is not a god of love but a sadist and despot[6]. Reformation attempts to justify all disease, war, pestilence and affliction as the purifying chastisements of an inscrutable Divine Will tell us more about the anxieties of Sixteenth Century European churchmen than the love of God[7]. The message of Calvinism, that we are morally helpless to resist sin but nevertheless justifiably dammed unless predestined to the Elect (and nobody can be sure who are the Elect) was and continues to be a recipe for depression and self-hatred[8].

Modern attempts to soften the Western doctrine of atonement by reinterpreting it as a salvific relational drama between God (transcendent) and God (immanent) still require that the sacrifice of Jesus was necessary for salvation. For example, Jürgan Moltmann in his book, 'The Crucified God' argues that within the Trinity, there is a history; 'Faith understands the historical event between the Father who forsakes and the Son who is forsaken on the cross in eschatological terms as an event between the Father who loves and the Son who is loved in the present Spirit of the love that creates life.'[9] Love here, involves experiencing godforsakenness, a sense of the annihilation of Being within God, I suppose this is the only form of pain that Moltmann considers the Trinity can enter into. I do not really understand why it is necessary to speculate upon the inner dynamics of the Trinity in order to meditate upon the sufferings of Jesus on the cross, unless one is trying to solve the Greek philosophical presupposition that God cannot suffer because God is eternal and unchanging. And why should we humans expend energy as Moltmann proposed, 'sowing in hope, self-surrender and sacrifice'[10], if love, death and the future salvation of the world is an internal matter between God the Father and God the Son?

As a feminist, my particular criticism of a sacrificial interpretation of the death of Jesus is coloured by its historical effect upon women. In the Latin tradition, certainly since the Fifth Century, sin has been inextricably associated with sex. According to Augustine, original sin is transmitted from generation to generation through the sex act and women, as daughters of Eve, literally bear the consequences (children, moral corruption, pain and mortality[11]). Tertullian, writing as early as the Second Century, castigated Christian women with the sentence:

'Do you not know that you are Eve?.. You are the devil's gateway... How easily you destroyed man, the image of God. Because of the death which you brought upon us, even the Son of God had to die.'[12]

Women, through virtue of their sex, were considered guilty of the death of Christ. To make satisfaction for their guilt, women were offered two forms of expiation, either in a spirit of passivity and obedience to bear the pain of childbearing and submit to their husbands or to transcend their sex and become like men through celibacy and ascetic practices.

The existential guilt of womanhood and the Christian emphasis on following Jesus the bridegroom on the way of the cross led to masochistic practices amongst medieval nuns and mystics. Sara Maitland cites in her essay, a hagiographical account of Rose of Lima (1586-1617) who was canonized in 1671:

'... to keep herself from sleep she suspended herself ingeniously upon the large cross which hung in her room... and should this fail she attached her hair (the one strand at the front which she had not shaved off) to the nail in the feet of her Christ so that the least relaxation would inflict terrible suffering upon her... Rose represented forcibly the necessity she felt of suffering this continual martyrdom in order to be conformable to her divine spouse.'[13]

Maitland maintains this form of self-inflicted penitential excess was not an isolated incident. She comments:

'Women flagellate themselves, starve themselves, lacerate themselves, kiss lepers' sores ... deform their faces with glass, with acid, with their own fingers; they bind their limbs, carve up their bodies,

51

pierce, bruise, cut, torture themselves. The most highly praised mystical writings use metaphorical imagery for these acts: women speak of Christ's rape of them, they abase themselves, abuse themselves ...What the hell is going on here?'[14].

One may well ask, particularly since female masochistic practices related to a self-sacrificing identification with the death of Jesus are not confined to the Middle Ages but have played a debilitating role in the lives of Christian women up to the present day.

Perhaps the most tragic example of this phenomenon in the contemporary West is to be found in cases of incest amongst pious religious families. In the Netherlands for example, the incidence of incest abuse is greatest amongst patriarchal families where a rigid sexual morality dominates. It is perhaps now well known that a girl whose identity is not fully formed is extremely vulnerable to sexual abuse from her father or male relatives. This vulnerability is heightened in families structured upon authoritarian patriarchal principles where women are considered morally weak and dangerous and are thus exhorted to be submissive and obedient to men, even in the area of sexual relations. When in such repressive situations a strict form of Christianity is practised, religion can increase the trauma. For in the eyes of the child the identity of the father is confused with images of an Almighty God Father demanding obedience and threatening judgement whilst Jesus becomes the role-model for her (loving?) self-sacrifice[15]. The wounds of self-hate, guilt-feelings, depression, nightmares, sexual rigidity or promiscuity and loss of faith which haunt incest victims cannot be overestimated. A pastor in a Dutch women's psychiatric hospital, after conducting research for a study into the problem, concluded that between 25% and 35% of the patients suffered from sexual abuse as children[16].

The question arises, is it possible to preach 'Christ crucified' without evoking destructive forms of guilt and masochism? The history of Christian missionary activity can be interpreted as the colonization of the hearts and minds of oppressed peoples through the ideological misuse of the Christian Gospel. Not only women, but Black slaves in the West Indies and Anti-bellum America, Indians in Latin America, Africans, peoples from the Indian Subcontinent and Asiatics were 'kept in their place' by a form of Christianity which engendered passivity and an ethic of self-sacrifice. We cannot assume that all these people

52

were simply so naive as to allow themselves to be brainwashed and pacified. Therefore the question about the appeal of the crucified Christ is a complex one. On the one hand, Jesus on the cross encouraged oppressed peoples to accept their suffering under their taskmasters as in some sense redemptive, but on the other hand the suffering Jesus gave them a sense of comfort, for God in Jesus understood their pain and grief and shared their heavy load.

In his book, 'The Anti-Christ', the Nineteenth Century philospher Friedrich Nietzsche argued that Christianity was and is a religion for slaves, for,'everything ill-constituted, rebellious-minded, under-privileged, all the dross and refuse of mankind'[17]. Nietzche's bitter invective against the morality and religion of German middle-class burghers should not distract us from his central point. We know from the Gospels that the original followers of Jesus were fishermen and social outcasts such as lepers, the demon possessed, taxcollectors and prostitutes. The first Christian theologian, Paul of Tarsus, was only an itinerant tentmaker. In her reconstruction of the earlist Christian missionary movement, Elisabeth Schüssler Fiorenza argues persuasively that the rapid spread of Christianity throughout the Roman Mediterranean world was the result of a role-revolt of the oppressed. Male and female slaves revolted against their legal inferiority by claiming equality in the Christian Body of Christ and upper-class Roman matrons revolted against their enforced restriction to the private sphere of the patrician household by opening their homes to the new movement and patronizing house-churches and itinerant preachers[18].

It would appear then, that the earliest Christian proclamation of a suffering prophet of God and the scandal of the cross, prompted social and even revolutionary impulses. The identification through analogy of persecuted early Christians with their suffering Jesus did not lead to masochism, dependency or powerlessness. Why was this? Rita Nakashima Brock points out, 'empathetic attunement prevents one person from inflicting suffering on another because the dignity and value of the other as a unique and distinct self is affirmed. Our ability to suffer with another empowers us, where possible, to stop suffering.'[19] In this sense, meditation upon a suffering Jesus-messiah prompted solidarity in the face of suffering, resistance to unnecessary suffering and strategies to survive through hope in a new liberated future. We can see these aspects beautifully expressed in the prayer of an old Black American slave woman:

'Come to we, dear Massa Jesus. De sun, he hot too much, de road am dat long and boggy and we ain't got no buggy for send and fetch Ooner (you). But Massa, you 'member how you walked dat hard walk up Calvary and aint't weary but tink about we all dat way. We know you ain't weary for to come to we.'

This prayer is cited in Jacquelyn Grant's book, 'White Women's Christ and Black Women's Jesus'. She comments, 'This slave woman did not hesitate to identify her pains and struggles with those of Jesus. In fact, the common struggle made her know that Jesus would respond to her beck and call.'[20]

In my opinion, in the discussion about the ideological and oppressive abuse of the doctrine of the atonement we have to distinguish clearly between descriptive and prescriptive theology. If suffering people choose to identify with Jesus on the cross and find there comfort, strength and inspiration to live, then the role of the theologian is to reflect upon these experiences of redemption. But when theologians, missionaries or preachers blame on a subjugated people or an inferiorized sex the sins that led to the death of Christ and demand penitential self-denial, the result is not redemptive. Rather, victims of human injustice are blamed for the sins of their oppressors and are loaded with a sense of interiorized guilt and self-hatred which saps the power of resistance and isolates creative vision, turning it in upon itself in the forms of a sense of inferiority, depression and even despair.

It may be argued that, whilst I have provided a psychological explanation of the function of the suffering Jesus in the lives of the poor and oppressed, I have not offered a theological doctrine of the cross. Indeed, I have argued that atonement and sacrificial doctrines are unacceptable. This is indeed the case. I do not believe that it is possible to encapsulate in a dogma what happened salvifically or within the Trinity when Jesus died at Calvary.

The New Testament provides a kaleidoscope of different metaphors and opinions to persuade readers of the redemptive significance of this event. According to the Johannine account, the Holy Spirit flowed into the world as the heart of Jesus was pierced by the spear and he, essentially speaking, ascended directly to God the Father. However, in the Markan account Jesus cried in dereliction, 'My God, my God, why hast thou foresaken me?' and died in divine abandonment. It was this event which led the Roman centurian to exclaim, 'Truly this was a son of God!' In the Epistle to the Hebrews, Jesus as the great High Priest Melchizedek, sacrificed his own blood and spinkled it upon the altar of the Holy of Holies in the Temple, thus replacing the Mosaic Covenant with a new one. However, in his first letter to the church at Corinth, Paul developed a line of argument based upon the notion that the death of Jesus on the cross is a scandal, a stumbling block to Jews and folly to Greeks, 'but to those who are called, both Jews and Greeks, Christ the power of God and the wisdom of God' (I Cor.1 v.24).

One could go on to list the four different categories of atonement doctrines in the New Testament, as delineated by J.F.Bethune-Baker[21], or to speculate upon the meaning of the Lukan Greek-hero Jesus prototype or the Pauline metaphor of cosmic reconciliation. However, I would argue that it is enough, theologically speaking, to assert with the witnesses to the crucifixion that as they stood and watched Jesus suffer and die the sky turned black, the mocking thieves and executioners became afraid but the almighty power of God was silent. After the resurrection, these same disciples realized that in the martyrdom of their prophet they had witnessed a divine mystery which could not be accommodated in Jewish theological or Greek philospohical categories, namely that God suffers with and for humanity to redeem her from injustice and death.

The Scandal of the Vulnerable God

That the love of God for humanity is so profound that God has chosen to share with human life in the vulnerable mode of suffering was and is a remarkable Christian insight. The disciples who first glimpsed this reality did not come to this conclusion on the basis of a logical syllogism based upon a doctrine of the Trinity or that Jesus Christ had two natures, human and divine. Rather, it was disclosed to them through an intense process of communal grief and ecstasy. However, Jesus had prepared the way for this spiritual revolution. Through his healing and exorcism ministry he had constantly emphasised the compassionate presence of God amongst the sick and unhappy. Further, he had associated the promised messianic feast of the Kingdom of God with the ingathering of all the poor, handicapped and

55

outcast. His words at the Last Supper, 'This is my body' and 'This is my blood of the covenant, which is poured out for many', stressed the presence of the prophet of God in the physicality of daily life, in bread, wine, body, blood, human friendship, love and even death.

However, Jesus never proclaimed the necessity of suffering. His ministry was life-affirming; he sought to eradicate pain and social distress and preach Good News to the poor and heavy hearted. That he could not finally avoid suffering and an early death is a tragedy and a prophetic exposure of the nihilstic tendencies of those who idolize power. It can be argued that Jesus believed that his action of directly confronting the Roman political and Jewish sacerdotal powers in Jerusalem would inaugurate an apocalyptic crisis in which God would overthrow the corrupted human power structures and come to reign directly. However I do not believe that we can enter into the consciousness of Jesus and fully understand his motives for setting into motion the confrontation which led to his passion and death. Nor can we reconstruct what he felt and believed from the fragmentary and disparate accounts of the Gospels. But we do know that these traumatic events led to a revolutionary religious insight amongst his followers, namely that God was present at the crucifixion, not as an impassive transcendental observer, but as actively sharing with the victim in a solidarity of suffering and grief.

It may be argued that my thesis that the first Christians believed in a God who suffered with Jesus does not square with the images of the glory and lordship of Jesus Christ found in the New Testament. I accept that the Early Church also proclaimed with some triumphalism, particularly in times of persecution, the resurrection and vindication of their Jesus-messiah but they always emphasised that their conception of God's power stood absolutely in contrast to Roman emperor worship. Thus for example, in the Johannine account of the trial of Jesus before the Roman Governor Pontius Pilate, Pilate rhetorically asked Jesus, 'So you are a king?' Jesus replied, 'You say that I am a king. For this I was born, and for this I have come into the world, to bear witness to the truth.' Pilate then asked, 'What is truth?' He received no reply from the Galilean carpenter who stood with crown of thorns before him (John 18 v.37-38).

If the first Christians did have a revolutionary conception of the nature of the God to whom Jesus bore witness, it was a short-lived revelation. The succeeding generations of bishop-theologians were by training and temperament inclined towards mainstream Greco-Roman philosophical categories. They saw their task as providing an intellectually satifying apologetic for Christian belief. The result was the paradoxical dogmas of the councils of Chalcedon and Nicea. For, it may be asked, how is it possible to defend the insight that God suffers (and can therefore change) if one's presupposition is that God is Aristole's 'Unmoved Mover' or Plato's 'Being beyond being'? The intellectual climate at the time of the councils is best described as Neo and Middle -Platonic. The Neo-Platonists 'One Supreme God' was conceived to be the ground of Being, perfect in form and substance, undifferentiated, indivisible, impassive, unaffected and without development, history or involvement[22].

To square this conception of God with the early Christian proclamation of a suffering God revealed in the crucifixion of a Jewish carpenter required mental gymnastics of the first order. The Church Fathers attempted to resolve the puzzle by positing two abstract conceptions. First, since God was conceived of as eternal, and therefore beyond time and space, it was necessary to argue that Jesus participated in divinity in order to claim that God participated in the death and resurrection of Jesus. Secondly, since God is wholly Other than humanity it was necessary to posit that Jesus possessed two natures, one human and one divine. To put it crudely, the human Jesus suffered and died, the divine Christ dwelling within the divine sphere of the Trinity remained unaffected.

Don Cupitt has argued that the doctrine of Chalcedon, (that Christ had two natures, each entire, united without confusion in one divine person, co-essential with Deity in his divine nature and co-essential with us in his human nature) is 'internally incoherent'. He asks; 'how one can intelligibly affirm that a single subject, the divine Word, possesses three sets of attributes, the set which comprise his divine nature, the set which comprise essential human nature and a set of contingent human attributes, when some of the attributes in the first set appear to be incompossible in a single subject with some in the other two sets?'[23] It may be that it is possible to approach the Chalcedon formula of 'truly God and truly man' as an existential symbol for the incarnation of the divine in our embodied selves. I shall explore this possibility in Chapter 6. However a symbol with endless

57

permutations for interpretation and exploration is quite different from a dogma which is considered to be the touchstone and test of religious orthodoxy. My point here is that it is not necessary to hold to the doctrine that Jesus of Nazareth was a (semi)divine being in order to believe that God was present in the mode of suffering at Calvary.

I have tried to show in this essay that the central theological insight of the Christian proclamation of the cross is that God is present and in loving solidarity with those who suffer unjustly at the hands of corrupt and violent people. This insight does not require an atonement doctrine, Jesus was not sacrificed as a guilt offering to pay for human sin nor do we have to continually repay our debt to Jesus by sacrificing ourselves. The divinization of Jesus Christ by the Church Fathers does not explain what happened on the cross; it only confuses the issue. If the Greco-Roman world was scandalized by the Christian message of a vulnerable God it only made the problem more intractable if one argued that Jesus was also in part divine. For one was then led inevitably into a docetist position, namely the belief that since God is incapable of suffering the divine nature of Jesus did not suffer and die.

I maintain that it is possible to believe that God was in Jesus reconciling believers to God's Self upon the cross without claiming the Jesus was uniquely divine or that a blood price was paid. It is possible for me to believe this because I believe that God did and does suffer. In other words, along with many other feminist theologians, I have rejected the Greek conception of the nature of God. I no longer believe that God is absolutely transcendent, the God I worship with my living is present in the universe, close by, indeed within me. This God is the source of birth, life and death (which is the process of the transformation of energy and matter into another state). This God is also the power of love and justice which is released in human relationships.

Such a God, who in a certain sense is immanent and embodied in the universe of time and space, energy and matter, cannot be a static or abstract principle. All living things are in a process of change and becoming, if growth stops then there is atrophy and death. In this sense, God can be conceived of as in a process of becoming, God also has a history with a past, a present and a future. Further, as Grace Jantzen has shown, such a God requires no intermediaries to understand pain and pleasure. If God is overall present; then God directly feels what all living beings feel and knows directly every thought and motive.[24]

Such a God may have identified with the mission, passion and death of Jesus and shared his humiliation and torture at the hands of unjust powers. To believe this requires a conception of God which is personal. It assumes that God can have relationships with humans and can share their hopes and sorrows. For this relationship to be described as loving however, it is necessay to take the following logical step and argue that God has chosen to abdicate divine power where humans freedom is concerned. Love requires a mutuality of concern and an equality of power. And love bonds, if the beloved suffers, the lover suffers too. Finally, to believe in a present, personal and loving God requires a belief in the vulnerability of God within the human situation.

One may go even further with this argument and say that God is not only vulnerable within the human situation per se, but also within the evolution and history of our planet, the Earth. This beautiful planet with its abundant variety of species depends upon an intricate network of eco-balances. Humanity since the Industrial Revolution, has been systematically undermining these balances through over- exploitation of our planet's natural resources and through pollution and unjust distribution of the natural economy. The future of our living planet is in jeopardy from human greed. Finally if we destroy our mother Earth, we shall not only destroy the human race but also the living presence of God upon and within our world.

Why God should choose to abdicate absolute divine power and share so intimately with human life and history is a mystery. According to the Johannine writings in the New Testament, God's nature is love. In his famous eulogy to the Christian conception of love, Paul wrote, 'Love bears all things, believes all things, hopes all things, endures all things. Love never ends...'[25]. But is love enough? To believe that God was present sharing the pain and grief of Jesus on the cross does not solve the problem of human evil. Why did God allow such a good man to be tortured and crucified? Where is the justice of God, which the prophet Amos described as a mighty rolling river? Jesus, whilst realising in the Garden of Gethsemane that his death was inevitable, finally cried out on the cross, 'my God, my God, why have you abandoned me!'

We are faced at this point with a theodicy problem, how can the goodness of God be justified in the light of evil? The classical Christian answer to this problem was based upon two central models. The first model is that of the Last Judgement as described in the Book of Revelation. In this terrifying scenario, destructive plagues are released upon the earth as Christ opens seven seals, pours out the seven bowls of God's wrath and finally six trumpets are sounded, the last inaugurates the coming of the four angels of death. An apocalyptic battle, the Armageddon then ensues between Christ and hideous beasts, a dragon, the Whore of babylon and the Anti-Christ. The elect Christians however, are gathered into the New Jerusalem where they worship God and Christ for ever[26].

The images of the Book of Revelation dominated the pysche of Medieval Europe. The belief in purgatory meant that no one could wholly escape the purifying fires of God's wrath. It is a misconception to think that the Reformation offered an escape from this nightmare. Luther and Calvin were as terrified of God's judgement as the German peasants who sold all that they had to buy indulgences for their dead relatives. Under the chapter heading, 'Calvin's Anxieties', William Bouwsma describes the existential angst that played such an important part in Calvin's life and writings and mirrored to a great degree the anxieties of the early Sixteenth Century. He cites two examples of Calvin's fear of judgement[26]. In his Commentary on Isaiah 10 v3, Calvin wrote; 'If the judgements of God are so dreadful on this earth, how dreadful will he be when he shall come at last to judge the world! All the instances of punishment that now inspire fear and terror are nothing more than preludes for that final vengeance which he will thunder against the reprobate.' In his Commentary on Psalm 32v.4 Calvin observed that, 'when, oppressed by the hand of God, the sinner feels he has to do with a judge whose wrath and severity contain innumerable deaths beyond eternal death.' Death beyond death, hell beyond human imaginings, this was Calvin's sense of the perfect justice of God.

The obsession with death and judgement which gripped Medieval Christendom is in my opinion, one of the most tragic failures of Christianity. During the periodic waves of the Black Death which swept across Europe decimating the population by 50% the people found no comfort in living or dying. The clergy and monks had become corrupted by wealth and almost illiterate, they could not expound the Book of Revelation from within its biblical or historical context, for the Book is the vision of John, an early Christian prophet who was forced to work as a slave in the stone quarries of Patmos as a punishment for his beliefs. His vision clearly alludes to the hope that God will finally punish the Nerodian and Domitian Emperor-worshipping Roman imperial cult and vindicate the persecuted Christians[27]. It is one of the greatest ironies of history that the emperor Constantine forcibly converted the Roman Empire to Christianity and claimed to have inaugurated the Millenium (the thousand year reign of Christ on earth which is described in John's vision). The angst and social unrest of the late Middle Ages was partly the result of a popular belief that the Millenium was drawing to its close and the Last Judgement was at hand[28].

I cannot accept that the revenge theology of John of Patmos should be the basis for a theodicy. It failed the Christians of the Middle Ages and although it has fuelled the speculations of various apocalyptic sects down through the ages, it is finally based upon an extremely pessimistic view of humanity and a wrathful image of God which I reject. A proper sense of the justice of God requires that we trust that the God of love shall finally bring all our good potentials to fruition. The shadow side of our personalities and the harm which we knowingly or unknowingly do to others is also a part of the history of the presence of God with us and finally it is a question of hope that the God who knows and feels everything in our hearts shall deal justly and mercifully with us.

A second Christian answer to the problem of evil in the world was based upon the transcendent conception of God which I have already described with reference to the Church Fathers. Here, God is conceived of as untouched by evil because God is eternal, beyond time and space, change and passion. The philosphical problem then arises, if God is perfect Goodness and absolute in Power, how does evil arise? Early Christians speculated with two solutions, either Satan as a fallen angel brought evil into the world, or Eve through her disobedience corrupted humanity and thus released mortality into the world. In both scenarios, God as the creator allowed evil, corruption and death to enter Paradise, but God was not held responsible for initiating evil only for punishing it. Some Christian Gnostic sects, took this line of reasoning to its logical conclusion and argued that since Satan or Eve was created by God, the potential for evil within them originated from the creator, therefore the creator is not the One Supreme God but a lesser god, the 'Demi-Urge'.

In my opinion, it is impossible to logically justify the Goodness of God in the light of human suffering and evil. However, one can choose between two sorts of conceptions of the nature of God. If one accepts the classical Neo-Platonist/Christian conception of a wholly Other transcendent God, then to a certain extent it is possible to believe that God is only Good. Evil, suffering and death belong to the realm of transcient life outside God. However, this God cannot be conceived of as in any way sharing human sorrow and pain. This God is impassive and uninvolved. The Church Fathers attempted to soften this conception of God by introducing the doctrine of the Trinity. However, this confusing dogma does not finally change the nature of the transcendent God because the Father, Son and Holy Spirit share the same essence and their relationship with each other is symbiotic and internal to the eternal sphere of reality.

A second conception of God is that God is personally present in the mode of loving solidarity, vulnerability and suffering within our human and planetary history. This is the theology which I have claimed to be grounded in the insights of those who stood at the foot of the cross. This God cannot be philosphically defended against the charge of final responsibility for evil. This God is wholly involved in human life and shares the consequences of human creativity and perversity. This God has abdicated power and chosen loving identification with the poor, the sick, the outcasts and the sinners. This God did not rise up in sublime justice and take Jesus down from the cross or strike his oppressors with thunderbolts from heaven. But this God felt the pain of Jesus and the grief of forsakenness.

I do not believe that when Mary the mother of Jesus stood for six hours at the foot of the cross and watched her son die in agony she understood this as an act of atonement for the sins of the world. Her son's crucifixion was a penal punishment. He had been found guilty of political sedition against the Roman Empire. Further, in many Jewish eyes crucifixion was proof that somebody was cursed by God, for how could God allow somebody to die in such excruciating pain and public humiliation unless he had committed an unpardonable sin? I am sure that Mary, as any mother would, believed in the innocence of her son and as such felt a mixture of anger, grief and powerlesness at his execution. Whether she felt the presence of God in those terrible hours we do not know, but I think so, because she had always believed in her son's prophetic mission to Israel.

The Roman governor, Pontius Pilate decreed that the legal charge against Jesus be written on a placard in Hebrew, Latin and Greek and nailed above his head. His sentence read, 'Jesus of Nazareth, King of the Jews'. According to the Johannine account, the chief priests lodged a complaint and requested that the charge be altered to, 'This man said, 'I am King of the Jews''. Pilate refused to soften the messianic claim. Whether he believed that Jesus was a serious contender to the Davidic throne or whether he wished to offend the Jewish leadership is unclear. In the context of the entire Johannine passion narrative a third interpretation is possible, namely that Pilate was deeply troubled by the execution of Jesus and also by his claims to another sort of truth and power.

According to the Johannine version, Mary shared her vigil at the cross with her sister, Mary the wife of Clopas, Mary Magdalene, and a male unnamed disciple, 'whom Jesus loved'[29]). The rest of the disciples had abandoned Jesus and fled into the night when the soldiers came to arrest him in the Garden of Gethsemane. Peter had denied knowing Jesus and was in hiding in Jerusalem. It was some of these men who later came to believe that their guilt was somehow paid for sacrificially by the death of Jesus.

Before he died, Jesus said to his mother, 'Woman, behold your son' and to the beloved disciple he said, 'Behold, your mother'. John tells us that from that time, the man took Mary into his home. It is an important point that rarely receives attention, that in John's version the last thoughts of Jesus before his death were upon the wellbeing of his mother. In a patriarchal society, a widow whose eldest son receives the death sentence, is in an extremely vulnerable social and economic situation. Jesus may have felt abandoned by his disciples and his Abba-God but he did not abandon his mother, nor she him. The love beyond judgement and death which connected mother and son and indeed Jesus with Mary Magdalene is the basis for the ecstatic resurrection reunion. Their bonds of love and faith in the mission of Jesus the prophet were finally stronger than their grief and anger at the apparent silence of God. Because they were prepared to watch and wait in the darkness they came to understand how God is present in the human condition. Therefore they could recognise each other when the sun finally dawned on the third day.

5

THE RESURRECTION AND HERSTORY

'Woman, why are you weeping?'

The popular secular view of the resurrection of Jesus of Nazareth is that it is 'only a myth'. Behind this rather innocuous statement lies a set of closely connected viewpoints which many people assume to be part and parcel of a modern philosophy of reality. If we examine these presuppositions their foundations begin to shake.

Firstly, the view that science disproves the possibility of a bodily resurrection. The medical and biological sciences, it is said, clearly demonstrate that physical life after death is impossible. Since nobody has ever been resuscitated after brain-death and presented themselves for thorough-going anatomical and psychological tests, the possibility of the resurrection is nil. Such a position appears to be common sense and based upon logical reasoning which has taken all the empirical evidence into account. I regard it as naive for it assumes that present-day sciences are totally reliable, unbiased and capable of comprehending all the complexities of the phenomenon we call Life. Indeed, science is given the status of a religion in which we can have absolute faith.

Many scientists however, hold a much more sceptical view of their disciplines than is popularly thought. For example, since the publication in 1900 of Planck's quantum mechanics, followed by Einstein's theories of relativity and Heisenberg's principle of probablity, physicists have become extremely cautious about making truth-claims. They point out that since matter is comprised ultimately of waves of energy which constantly change their patterns of composition and which it is impossible to objectively study because of the influence of the observer, we can only posit theories of the relationship of one body to another. Further, it is not possible for a physicist to ascertain at the same time the position of a sub-atomic particle and its speed. So we could say that present-day research into the fundaments of existence practically means that scientists are bounded to one plane of reality, either time or space. In our daily lives we must act as if we understand how things are related to each other, if we do not use practical commonsense we cannot survive. But, philosophically speaking we understand very little. We cannot even comprehend the paradoxical relationship of time and space within one nucleus of one cell of our bodies. There is a mystery at the heart of modern science[1].

A second viewpoint, closely connected with the idolatry of science, is that we live in a mechanical universe where cause and effect constitute a continuum. Human history, it is said, also obeys this law. There can be no miracles, no supernatural interference with this ordering of reality. Here we are confronted with two viewpoints that are often confused with each other. The first is the softer empirical viewpoint that we can deduce the effect of something from observation and experience based upon the evidence of our senses. So for example, if I place an egg in a pan and set it on the gas, then I can be sure that the water will heat up and boil, the egg will cook and I can eat it for my breakfast. If for some reason this does not happen, then I can look for the cause of the problem and rectify it. If the gas does not come on then I know that there is a leak or the supply has been cut off, so I ring the Gas Board and ask for a repair. But one thing is absolutely certain, if the gas burns the water will boil at 100 degrees Centigrade.

This kind of cause and effect relationship is straightforward. From our experience we can deduce certain contingent laws of nature. I say 'contingent' because since Newton we have come to realise that for every law there is an exception and in any case the causal nexus is forever changing. There may come a time when the sun does not come up every morning, for example if her nuclear activity diminishes and she becomes a red giant. However for the present we can live as if it is a natural law that spring follows winter.

However if the contingent and limited horizons of the empirical viewpoint are not accepted we encounter what I would call hard determinism. For example when the Post-Christian feminist thelogian, Daphne Hampson argues that the causal nexus precludes the possibility of a resurrection she is in my opinion in danger of dogmatising empirical science[2]. The experience of cause and effect should not be turned into an ideology; it is not a self-evident reality such as the tautology a square has four right angles. In particular, persons are not robots whose behaviour or destiny can be programmed in advance. For one hundred years the new science of pyschology has attempted to measure human behaviour, judgements, motivations and deviations using biological and sociological tools but the fact remains that it has not proved possible up to the present to produce an adequate explanation of what an emotion is, how it is caused, how it is felt and how to predict its effect. And where is the seat of the mind to be found? Is it in the genetic makeup of DNA, in the 50% of the brain we apparently do not use, in the bowels, in the heart?

We are faced then with another mystery, that of the psyche. Perhaps the most that we can say is that we, as material physical beings, think and feel, that our matter has a sort of consciousness. In the infinite variety and complexity of the universe it is so that upon the earth energy has become living matter and matter has become self-reflective and feels itself. Confronted with this sort of description of a human being, who transcends herself in her immanence, it becomes extremely problematical to state categorically the relationship of death as a cause with its effect on the self. So I hold to the position of the great Christian philosopher and sociologist Ernst Troeltsch, that the opposite of supernaturalism is not Enlightenment dogmatism but qualified relativism. We must relativise our truth claims and reject claims to absolute knowledge.

It can be argued that Troeltsch also said that there can be no unique events in history such as the resurrection of Jesus. Yes he did write that[3], I do not think he was perhaps enough of a relativist, but then he lived before the dropping of the atomic bomb on Hiroshima and the Holocaust of the Jews in Europe. These events, in order of magnitude of horror, cruelty and abuse of power were at the time unique in history and I pray shall forever so remain. Relativism cuts both ways, one cannot say categorically that the resurrection of Jesus did not happen or that it did. If for good reasons one chooses to believe in the probability of the resurrection then that faith must be coloured by a good deal of agnosticism. Agnosticism literally means unknowing and it is precisely in our accepting that there are things that we do not fully know or understand that it makes it possible for us to discover and create new things.

A third connected viewpoint is that science disproves myths. Myths are popularly understood to be fairy stories, folk-tales, primitive

66

science or collective fantasies, in other words, the opposite of hard facts. However, anthropologists tell us that myth-making was the third stage in the evolution of a tribal identity; that first came the sense of the cosmic powers, and then the dance and finally the myth[4]. Myths developed as communal linguistic symbols to order the experience of a people and place that experience in the context of a relationship with the cosmos, nature, the social structures and experimental knowledge. Peter Berger has described mythologies as the sacred canopies which people erected over their heads to protect them from anomie, that is, meaninglessness, dread and chaos[5].

The question is, have we modern Westerners outgrown myth? The secularist would answer, 'yes'. With modern technology and the communications explosion we do not need myths anymore, we can control our environment, we are autonomous individuals who can think for ourselves, God the transcendent Subject is dead. I do not agree. The sterility, loneliness and angst of the modern life in the city convinces me that no amount of information technology can enable individuals to place themselves meaningfully in society or the universe. We need a language, rich enough in symbol and metaphor to bind us into a sense of a cultural identity and destiny, to ground us in Being and Becoming. The loss of myth and the sacramental world-view has left us with only a boring and repetitive literalism; language has become newspeak, statistical analysis, bureaucratic jargon and political slogans. Disaffected youth, disinhereted of their right to poetry and the cosmic powers, have given up on language and returned to the beat of the dance. Sallie McFague has warned that literalism leads to fundamentalism in religion as believers forget how to read their Scriptures as metaphor and parable[6]. The aridity of religion and market-force politics in the contemporary West is, in my opinion, the fruit of the powerlessness of the people when their vision perishes.

But how can we reinstate myth as a step in liberation? We cannot go back in time to a world where room to play in a divine space and weave communal stories was an essential element of daily life[7]. Nor do I think it is correct, to sit behind a word processor, as Mary Daly does, and type up a new myth. Perhaps, as individuals we can create our own fantasies or, as Sallie McFague recommends, experiment with new heuristic models for God[8]. But these are not myths born of communal experience, grounded in the history of a people. I have come to the conclusion that the best step is to reclaim the myths of my own cultural and historical tradition. Some of these myths are patriarchal and have exercised powerful cultural control over women. These myths can only be reclaimed through a process of deconstruction, grappling with the ideological and psychological oppressiveness of such myths is a form of emancipation; to conquer a myth is a form of reclaiming it. However, my concern here is with the myth of the resurrection, which, far from being patriarchal, offers an evocative and powerful symbol of life springing out of death, of human hope conquering injustice and terror.

The question still remains however, how do I know that this myth is grounded in reality? How can I be sure that it is authentic, that it is a genuine reflection of how life and death, good and evil, humanity and the presence of God interact? I have already said that I cannot categorically know if the resurrection of Jesus occurred or not. I can however believe that it was probable and take the risk of faith where knowledge falls short. This is the position that the feminist theologian, Rosemary Radford Ruether took in her public debate with Daphne Hampson. She argued that if the resurrection was 'only literally true' it would simply be an oddity, but that in fact its significance lies in its 'metaphorical' and paradigmatic meaning[9]. Hampson replied with rigorous logic, that if Ruether was actually saying that the resurrection is 'only a myth' then she was denying the reality and efficacy of the resurrection and it would be better to scrap it in favour of a feminist myth. One sees here the impasse that is reached if myth and history are played off against each other as if they constituted fiction and fact.

If there is one fact about myth, it is that it emerges from history. Something offering a liberational new disclosure of life happened in the experience of a group of grieving disciples. In seeking to give it a form they wrestled with language, a language steeped in their Jewish and Hellenistic context. Finally they found a way of expressing those traumatic events; God had raised the prophet Jesus from the dead and death has lost its sting. A symbolic story was born which was to prove revolutionary in the Greco- Roman world. This myth, once it was formulated, took on its own life, simultaneously reshaping culture and adapting to different cultural contexts. Whether Jesus literally rose from the dead or not, the myth arose in history and has to a great extent shaped Western history for two thousand years. The legitimate question to ask, then, is not one of facticity but of relevance.

The Christian churches have traditionally indoctrinated their children into accepting the creeds as mystical formulas for salvation. The mystification of belief and the absolutism of the authority of the clergy finally led to an intellectual rebellion in the Enlightenment. I stand in the Enlightenment tradition to the extent that I claim the right to think through religion for myself. If then, I choose to believe in the resurrection of Jesus of Nazereth it must be because I perceive that this faith has some kind of relevance for my situation and experience. This religious myth must speak existentially to my religious search for salvation and liberation.

Further, that relevance must have some connection with my politics as a feminist. It is not enough that I eccentrically go my own way to pursue some sort of personal mystical satisfaction. As a feminist the personal is political; my ethics, life-style, ideals and work are rooted in the context of a wider movement of liberation. I try to be in solidarity with my sisters, even if differences in context, race, class, culture and religion mean that our struggle for freedom emerges from our diversity. I am committed at the very least to dialogue with other women suffering from various forms of oppression and powerlessness. So, if I choose to appropriate the myth of the resurrection and I do not wish to be intellectually or politically dishonest, I must be prepared to give some account of its relevance for me within the wider context of feminism. If I cannot do this, then I really should stop believing, for my faith becomes nothing but an anomaly; unauthentic and probably a form of self-delusion or spiritual arrogance.

How then can I approach the liberational relevance of the resurrection as a feminist theologian? In the classical Christian tradition, such as one finds in the Apostles Creed there are three vertical movements. After his death Jesus descended into hell, then on Easter morning he ascended to the earth and finally on Ascension Day, he ascended into heaven to sit in glory at the right hand of God the Father. These three tiers of hell, earth and heaven reflect the ancients' sense of reality. In both Jewish and Hellenistic thought-worlds reality was divided spatially. Galileo. in demonstrating that the world is round and revolves around the sun, inaugurated the death of the vertical movement. More recently, the three movements have been interpreted chronologically, in time rather than space. The movements then describe a series of events within the God the Trinity which are actually eternal but were played backwards into time as an anticipation of the Eschaton, the end of history. The descent into hell is then interpreted as the nadir of God through his Son. Jesus as the so-called 'kenotic' Christ identifies himself out of love for the Father with the dead damned. The resurrection is the eschatological moment of New Creation. The new reality of the Second Adam for a brief time appears upon the earth anticipating the glorification of 'Man' in the New Heaven and Earth. Finally Christ is reunited with the Father in an eternal symbiosis which is the inner reality of human and cosmic history.

This sort of theology is particularly prevalent in the German schools of Barth, Moltmann and Pannenberg. I find it too speculative. How can a theologian claim to know in detail what happens after death or what constitutes the inner dynamics of the Selfhood of God! The biblical accounts of the resurrection appearances of Jesus are vague, do not correlate with each other and give an overall impression of shock bordering on angst. All that we can glean from the accounts is that, three days after his crucifixion, Jesus was witnessed to be alive by some of his disciples, notably Mary of Magdala and Peter of Capernaum. Their experiences generated a new religion based upon the continuing presence of Jesus as a living Christ-Person who could be experienced through the Holy Spirit. So it was that the Pharisee Saul of Tarsus met Jesus in a vision some years later. He based his claim to the spiritual authority to be an apostle on this encounter[10].

The development of Patristic dogma during the first six centuries of the Church was a process of codification and finally canonization of what were regarded as orthodox interpretations of these events. We should not forget that the ecstatic dance came first. Gradually the experiences of ecstasy were brought under some kind of order with the development of ritual, that is liturgy and a clergy to service it. During this process of ecclesiastical expansion structure and authority took precedence over prophecy and messianism. Bishops were locked in a desperate struggle on the one hand to provide an intellectual and moral apology for Christianity in the light of Stoicism and Neo-Platonism, and on the other hand to suppress heterodox forms of Christianity which did not accept their authority. The final and absolutely binding

70

interpretation of the myth was however, not so much a triumph for the bishops as for the emperors who required orthodoxy of belief and practice to legitimise their dual claim to the delegated authority of Christ Pantocrator and to the Imperium.

Messianic Hope and the Prophetic Dead

When I suggest reclaiming the myth of the resurrection as a symbolic focus for modern life I do not wish to propose returning to the Councils of Chalcedon and Nicea. The misappropriation of the myth to prop up ideologies of absolutism or patriarchy is in my opinion blasphemous. Neither do I wish to speculate upon a demythologization of the three movements of Christ in time and space. Rather,I am simply arguing that we try to believe that God acts in history with dynamic efficacy to justify the victims of oppression, torture and execution, that the message, goodness and presence of a prophet such as Jesus of Nazereth cannot be obliterated by human evil. God raised her prophet from the dead. This is succinctly encapsulated in the words of Rosemary Ruether, 'The memory (of the martyr) becomes stronger than the powers of death and gives people hope that the powers of death can be broken'[11].

In my opinion, such a hope requires a far greater act of faith than to simply believe it is possible for a dead and mutilated corpse to be revivified. To believe in the resurrection challenges us to a passionate commitment to Life. We are inspired to assert in the face of all experience to the contrary that the faceless politicians, international bankers and diplomats who control the economies of our world shall not have the power to allow a child to starve in Africa or a tribe to be exterminated in the Amazon. No one could believe such a thing unless she has first struggled with her own fear of death and suffering and has reached an integrated sense of her own vulnerability and power. Belief in the resurrection requires moral maturity and a wisdom that can probe beneath the surfaces of newspapers and cities to the heart of Life.

To choose to believe in the resurrection is not a cop-out but a diving into the realities of history. If we can hope that our struggle for justice will be vindicated, even beyond our own lifetime, then we have no

71

excuse for passivity or defeatism. However lonely, frustrated or angry I may feel as a feminist living and trying to work in a man's world, I can nurture my spiritual resources of hope. Simply because one is not thanked, rewarded, promoted or even listened to does not mean that one's actions are futile or crazy. In the presence of God we can rise again; the powers of darkness can never overcome the sisters and brothers of radical hope.

If we reclaim the belief in the resurrection using this kind of approach, there will be far-reaching consequences for a contemporary christology. The uniqueness of Christ is not central to such an interpretation, rather the emphasis lies upon the power and presence of God to defeat evil and death and our ability to recognise this. But how can we develop the sensibility to believe in the prophetic dead? The theologian John Mbitu described how in the African sense of reality, people feel the presence of their near ancestors as the living-dead. The living-dead stay with their families in the dynamic present advising them on all important matters. They finally slip away into 'Tene' time, the world of spirits and 'collective immortality', when their names and deeds are forgotten[12]. In the sceptical West, animistic and shamanistic beliefs tend to be regarded as 'primitive' and hence inferior. Nevertheless, we too recall the living-dead in the sense of reading their letters, books, poetry and political agendas, singing their songs, contemplating their art and recalling memories of them with friends.

The influence of the good dead, in Christian terms the communion of saints, depends upon memory and recollection. But many of the good have been forgotten or indeed their presence from our history has been erased or silenced. This is pre-eminently true of women, who in the androcentric mind-set of reality were only regarded as the natural 'backdrop' to the public male world of culture (Bernadette Brooten[13]). In her book, 'In Memory of Her', Elizabeth Schüssler Fiorenza uses the tools of biblical criticism, sociology, linguistics and women's history to break through the silence of the New Testament text concerning the praxis and authority of the first Christian women[14]. She argues that the theological meaning of the Jesus Movement and the Early Christian Missionary Movement cannot be grasped until a hermeneutic of feminist suspicion is applied to the New Testament canon. Hidden beneath the text and in clues in the text is the silenced

72

suffering and power of our spiritual foremothers. To recover and retell their story for Womenchurch is to reclaim women's memory, a memory which challenges the epistemological and religious framework of Western power and knowledge[15].

An example of a forgotten and denigrated woman who has finally been remembered by women and now haunts the male Church establishment is Mary of Magdala. In the Christian tradition she has been imaged as a repentant prostitute. In medieval France a cult developed around her, she fulfilled perhaps a compensatory role over against Mary the Virgin Mother of Jesus, the Queen of Heaven[16]. In the New Testament however, she is nowhere described as the 'magna peccatrix', rather she was a disciple who, in all four Gospels is given a unique status as the first witness and authorised proclaimer of the resurrection. She is in the words of St.Augustine, 'the apostle of the apostles'. It is then suprising to read in the paplical 'Declaration Against the Ordination of Women' that Peter is given this status and that indeed only male priests can represent the Person of Jesus Christ[17].

This forgetfulness concerning the apostolic status of Mary Magdalene is not limited to the Roman Catholic Curia. The Greek Orthodox theologian Kallistos Ware quotes with approval the opinion of the French Calvinist Jean-Jacques von Allmen:

'The New Testament, in spite of the chance of total renewal which it provides for women as well as men, never testifies that a woman could be, in a public and authorized way, representative of Christ. To no woman does Jesus say, 'He who hears you hears me.' To no woman does he make the promise to ratify in heaven what she has bound or loosed on earth. To no woman does he entrust the ministry of public preaching. To no woman ... etc, etc...'[18].

If one tries to reconstruct how this suppression of memory may have developed, suprising facts emerge. Paul of Tarsus, writing to the church in Corinth, claimed that the risen Jesus first appeared to Cephas (Peter) and afterwards to the twelve male disciples[19]. As Paul was not a witness to these events one can surmise that somebody gave him this information. Indeed, since Paul was not a disciple of Jesus of Nazareth, we must assume that all of his historical knowledge about the original Jesus Movement was second-hand. In his letter to the Galatians, Paul did in fact admit that it was taught to him by Peter in Jerusalem[20].

In 1945 at Nag Hammadi in Upper Egypt, a hoard of 52 leather-bound books were discovered in a buried stone jar. The books are gospels which were buried by the monks of Chenoboskia in the desert sands. Athanasius bishop of Alexandria had commanded the burning of all the gospels which were not recognised as canonical in his Easter letter of 367. The Pachomian monks as guardians of traditions from the 1st century thought otherwise. Thanks to their passive resistance to Roman imperial and ecclesiastical authority, we now have access to a range of extra-biblical Christian gnostic writings which circulated in the Middle-East before heterodoxy was suppressed. Amongst the gospels are the 'Gospel of Thomas', the 'Gospel of Philip' and the 'Pistis Sophia'. These texts together with the 'Gospel of Mary' (Magdalene) which had been discovered in 1896 in Cairo, describe Mary of Magdalene as the most intimate disciple of Jesus and claim that he taught her secret revelations after his resurrection. According to the Gospel of Mary, after Jesus ascended, Peter began to challenge her spiritual authority. At one point she was reduced to tears and said,

'My brother Peter, what do you think? Do you think that I thought this up myself in my heart? Do you think I am lying about the Saviour?'

Levi intervened in the dispute and said, 'Peter, you have always been hot-tempered.... If the Saviour made her worthy who are you to reject her?'[21]

On the basis of the various extra-canonical Christian gospels it would seem reasonable to surmise that Mary of Magdalene was extremely influencial in some of the earliest churches, that she was a preaching missionary founding communities which passed on her memories of Jesus. Her name came to be associated in the 1st Century with heterodox Christian communites who challenged the ecclesiastical and theological interpretation of the orthodox bishops claiming to speak for the Petrine apostolic tradition. Since Mary of Magdalene is nowhere mentioned in the letters of Paul one can only surmise that either he did not know of her or that he took Peter's cause in the struggle for apostolic authority. Finally her memory was erased by orthodoxy with the canonization of certain Scriptures and the suppression of alternative witnesses. For myself, the resurrected memory of Mary of Magdala as the first Christian witness of the power of God to defeat the death of a good prophet is a source of inspiration and female authority. I shall not forget her.

To choose to believe in the messianic efficacy of our spiritual ancestors does not depend upon a doctrine of Christ as the unique revelation of God. Further, it is not self-evident that if one believes in the power of God to raise the dead and vindicate the martyred prophet one must logically believe in the divinity of Christ. I do accept that the earliest Christians continued to believe and practise the way of the Kingdom of God because they experienced the living presence of their Jesus through the Holy Spirit. Further that for the women and men of the original Palestinian Jesus Movement, the experience of the resurrection of their crucified prophet was the basis for their evangelical enthusiasm. They expressed this enthusiasm by claiming that since God had raised Jesus from the dead they no longer accepted the lordship of the Roman emperor. Jesus was their 'kyrios' and the days of Rome were numbered.

As a feminist, I find the lordship of Christ an alienating belief. From a psychological point of view, my concern is with my female subjectivity; what does it mean to be and act as a female subject in a world where men have always defined femininity? How can I begin to feel and think from my authentic woman-self, how can I develop an integrity based upon the truths of my own embodied being? Christianity cripples this quest if I can only approach God through a superordinate male Lord who sits above my head on a throne of power and majesty. Does salvation require abasement and female self-denial before 'the Lord'? I do not believe so. The idolatry surrounding the lordship of Christ developed out of the practice of emperor worship. Christians began to literally copy the iconography and cult of the emperor at precisely the same time that the emperors adopted Christianity as the imperial religion[22]. It is absurd that such pagan forms of absolutism should take precedence over the evangelists accounts of Jesus, the prophet who ate with taxcollectors, prostitutes and sinners. How one can theologically relate the Johannine account of the Last Supper when Jesus wrapped a towel around his waist and washed his disciples' feet with many of our triumphalistic Victorian hymns? Could it be that the ideology of imperial Rome and Byzantium finally appropriated and subtly inverted the message of the Gospel?

I have argued that belief in the resurrection of Jesus of Nazareth is not necessarily irrational. Further I have tried to show how the

75

symbolic meaning of such an event may provide a platform for a vibrant and liberating form of contemporary spirituality. I have, on theological and feminist grounds rejected the classical dogmatic interpretation of the resurrection as proof of the unique divinity of Christ. The question remains, if I chose to emphasise the redemptive power of messianic prophecy without worshipping Christ as God, am I a Christian or 'only a humanist'? Daphne Hampson has argued that feminists who revere the teaching and praxis of Jesus but who do not proclaim his unique divinity are not Christians. She writes, 'To be concerned simply for Jesus' message which anyone could have preached and is now acknowledged quite independently of the person who preached it, is not to hold a Christian position. It is to hold a humanist position'[23].

I wish to take issue with this prescription, for it assumes christology is monolithic. In the last thirty years biblical scholarship has demonstrated clearly that the entire New Testament may be considered as a record of different christological approaches and beliefs. Further, church historians, liberation and feminist theologians have traced numerous conflicting tendencies throughout Christian tradition and history[24]. It is possible to delineate various trajectories; for example, Rosemary Ruether has found three: androgynous christologies, spirit christologies and masculinist christologies[25]. This is however a simplification. Christologies are intimately connected with context and also the sort of aspirations for salvation a community have. Christians tend to emphasise either personal salvation, or social salvation or cosmic salvation, but sometimes a mixture of the three. Also, the orthodox winners in the struggle for authority in the Church have tended to stress forms of christology which legitimate hierarchy through derived powers whilst heterodox and so-called heretical Christians have read the Gospel accounts as a witness to a radical destabilising messianism.

To choose therefore, to interpret the life and significance of Jesus using contemporary experience and concerns as my starting point is not illegitimate. If my thinking is coloured by Process Thought, Liberation Theology, Post-Modernism and Feminism it is not necessarily less Christian than Martin Luther's appropriation of Meister Eckhart, the Devotio Moderna, Renaissance discoveries and German nationalism. Christologies become irrelevant if they do not speak to

76

the experiences of God and salvific aspirations of the Christian communities from which they emerge. It is my contention that many of the forms of christology with which my generation of girls were raised are in fact meaningless or redundant. The reconstruction of christology requires that first of all women theologians make a serious and thorough reflection upon their own search for salvation. If we cannot square our Christianity with our own life stories then our theology is fundamentally dishonest.

Does this finally mean that systematic christology is to be rejected? Manuela Kalsky has argued that women theologians cannot sit up in an ivory tower and construct a new universally binding christology. Rather, since christologies are contextually-bounded, it is time to develop a new methodology based upon a recognition of fundamental differences. We must learn to express our christology through the medium of dialogue[26]. A Ghanaian woman farmer will not have the same image of Jesus as a Korean woman factory-worker or a white middle-class European feminist theologian. The most we can do is share our life-experiences and beliefs, that is, in the words of Nelle Morton, 'to hear each other into speech'[27]. But will this lead to a sort of post-modernist madness where christologies become so relativised that they finally lose their ethical and salvific content? I do not think so, provided that two things are borne in mind.

Firstly, the final test for a christology is that it must be grounded in a dialogue between the earliest Christian accounts of the life-praxis, death and resurrection of Jesus of Nazareth and the search of contemporary faith-communities for a relevant messianic spirituality. Secondly, that we do not forget that the imminent Kingdom of God which Jesus proclaimed is a message about the destabilising presence of God in history which can only be grasped through passionate participation in the search for salvation. Even dialogue about christology could become another form of literalism, of dead words, if those who dialogue have never danced to the rhythmn of the celebration of Life and resurrection. If I cannot taste my freedom and sense my victory then my christology will not be a personal testimony but an abstract theological discourse based upon the categories of homoousios, hypostasis, justification by faith and the sanctification of the elect.

77

Ecstasy and Effort: Celebrating and Renewing Life

As I bring this chapter to a close, I realise that there is one serious criticism which can be aimed at this reflection, namely that I have reduced belief in the resurrection to a psychological function. Am I simply saying feminist Christians, and all those involved in struggles for justice, need to believe in the resurrection as the vindication of the just martyr in order to give them courage and hope? Perhaps this is partly true; belief in the resurrection does compensate emotionally for our feelings of vulnerability in the face of suffering and evil. Anyone who has seriously entered into the spirit of Holy Week, sitting at the Last Supper, watching the agony and betrayal in Gethsemane, listening to the trials before the Sanhedrin and Pilate and meditating through the long night at the foot of the cross knows with what a sense of relief and joy the rising sun on Easter Sunday is welcomed. The sunrise picnics, blessing of children, baptisms, music, flowers and dancing witness to a collective sense of a crisis overcome as much as to a set of religious beliefs.

From a theological perspective, Christianity has always maintained that the life and crucifixion of Jesus can only be properly understood in retrospect, from the event of the resurrection. This is a problem for many contemporary theologians who have such intellectual difficulties with a belief in the resurrection. However, modern realism also has its dangers; to focus exclusively upon the passion and cross can lead to utter darkness and despair. For example, Jon Sobrino describes Jesus as a prophet who, in order to purify religion from its idolatrous accretions, purposely sets out to go to Jerusalem to die. Jesus commits a sort of theological suicide, abandoning himself to 'the monstrous power of negation'[28]. Similarly, there is a tendency in feminist liberation theology to describe the death of Jesus as a kind of idealistic anarchism, Jesus as the Angry Young Feminist makes the ultimate mistake in underestimating the powers of patriarchy. I do not find this exclusive concentration upon death liberational or Good News. If we focus our faith entirely upon self-sacrifice and destruction we are in danger of cultivating a cult of sado-masochism and necrophilia, which is precisely the criticism Mary Daly levelled against patriarchal Christianity[29].

I would suggest therefore, that the belief in the resurrection is a necessary psychological balance to belief in the cross. Christianity offers a myth which holds in creative tension the two poles of human existence, life and death. If the dialectic is undermined one is left with either desparing nihilism or triumphalistic supernaturalism. However, to argue for psychological balance in religion is not to reduce religion to psychology. The word salvation means wholeness and healing. This is not simply a psychological term but rather salvation is an integrative model which includes the entire embodied person in her relationship with the world.

Celebrating resurrection in our lives and the lives of our foremothers and fathers is a transformative process requiring creative imagination and a collective sense of what is of ultimate concern in our daily experiences. We do not have to be bound to dogma to give this form and expression. The biblical accounts of the witness of the resurrection of Jesus are poetic and dream-like. Rita Nakashima Brock has described them as a collective visionary-ecstatic imaging[30]. Whatever the status of the experiences behind the text, one thing is clear, the genre of faith is metaphor and experiment not the dead letter of literalism or fundamentalism. The writer D.H.Lawrence realised this more than 60 years ago when he wrote his novella, 'The Man Who Died'[31]. Lawrence speculated upon the resurrection of Jesus. In his account Jesus returned from the dead to demonstrate his rejection of his old religion based upon celibacy and rigid asceticism. Jesus undergoes a process of healing and finally makes his way to Egypt where he falls in love with a priestess of Isis. For Lawrence, this symbolized 'the resurrection of the flesh', the birth of a fully embodied religion which celebrates the erotic power of life. Lawrence was certainly not a feminist, thus it is all the more extraordinary that he should use the myth of the resurrection to anticipate the feminist concern for the embodiment of the spirit and the reclaiming of sexuality from the Augustinian obsession with original sin and death.

The novella of Lawrence is only one example of how the myth of the resurrection can be reappropriated in the present. The feminist theologian Susan Thistlethwaite offers a quite different response; she writes, 'Over the years I have learned that if Jesus rose anywhere for me, he rose in the survivors of abuse. This is what the resurrection means to me - as the words that make up the acronym VOICES state: Victims Of Incest Can Emerge Survivors'[32]. Belief in the resurrection is a particular way of looking at the world, a window on reality. Personally, my belief in the resurrection is rather mundane, it concerns how I interpret my daily life. The fact that somehow I manage to get through a day as a feminist theologian with some self-confidence, integrity, hope and vision intact is my resurrection. I rise up and am renewed in the presence of God in spite of everything.

THE INCARNATION AND THE QUEST FOR FEMALE SUBJECTIVITY

'But Mary kept all these things,
pondering them in her heart'[1]

When I had pastoral responsibility for a congregation, the coming of the Christmas Season evoked deep feelings both of pleasure and anxiety. Pleasure because I love the traditional English Christmas atmosphere. Christmas trees, fairy lights, carol singers, tinsel, holly, candles, presents and plum pudding are still part of an elusive magical world which has haunted me since childhood. Perhaps it is the innate longing for innocence, security and harmony, for Paradise lost.

However, as a professional Baptist minister I was faced every Advent with a problem which is shared by all contemporary Western clergy, namely how to compete with the entertainment industry. How could I think up and create such an attractive Christmas programme that my congregation would prefer to come to a Candlelight Carol Service rather than listen to the soothing 'peace and goodwill to all men' theme sung by countless pop stars on a live Christmas TV show. In the face of the secularisation or repaganisation of Christmas different confessional strategies have evolved. For example the Roman Catholic and Anglican churches try to insist that the Christmas Eve Mass/ Eucharist is compulsory for members. In practice this has led in some churches to an increasingly unpleasant situation. Drunken people, apparently seeking to regress into their infancy through the medium of music, candles and incense crowd into the church to sleep, fight or work themselves up into a maudlin state. In the Protestant Free Churches a service is held on Christmas Day. Here the strategy to attract members appears to be increasingly one of amusing the children with a Toy Service which convieniently fits in between the family rituals of giving presents around the Christmas tree and Christmas dinner.

If Christmas is difficult for contemporary clergy it is exhausting for women. Who mixes the plum pudding, shops for the holiday, saves up and buys the presents, makes the nativity clothes, invites and entertains the relatives, comforts and separates fractious children, cooks the Christmas dinner and herds the family off to church, rushes back and tries to rescue the turkey, arranges the table, serves the family, clears up and so on? These extra duties have become social expectations irrespective of religion. If one asks why women should make the extra effort to get the family to church on Christmas Day the traditional liturgical answer is in order to worship a new born boy god with the kings and shepherds and angels. For many thinking Christian women this romantic answer is becoming jaded. They may love their sons but they try not to worship them. Further, the nativity story they read in the Gospel of Luke speaks of a baby born to a poor unmarried mother in a hovel. A few peasant shepherds were there. The rest is Lucan commentary aimed at showing that Jesus was the long awaited Jewish Davidic Messiah which Luke illustrated using mythological motifs.

The pietistic sentimentalisation of Christmas is a Christian Victorian heritage which has led to the secularisation of Christmas and not vice versa. The churches should not condemn people for confusing God with Father Christmas or Santa Claus, or imagining the baby Jesus as a smiling white toddler with a halo and a woolly lamb. The fault lies in the failure of the Western churches to create the theological depth and practical steps necessary to ensure that Christmas is a holy day (holiday). For example, if Christmas is to be a proper time for spiritual reflection upon the mystery of the incarnation for women, then the Church needs to initiate an emancipatory practice which relieves the social and religious pressures which have conspired to make Christmas for women a time of extra care, effort and work.

The Male Logos and the Maleness of God

In my opinion, the forgetfulness that the church exhibits towards its female believers around the Christmas season is the consequence of a deeper theological malaise. It is not simply that women are excluded from a positive role in the nativity story because they cannot hope to

82

imitate Mary as virgin mother of Christ. It is rather that the doctrine of the incarnation does not directly address the female sex. Whilst the Chalcedon dogma that Jesus Christ was 'truly God and truly man' can be interpreted to mean that Jesus was a truly divinized human, Church doctrine and practice has used the formula to legitimise male supremecy in authority and even in nature. The Greek philosophical categories used by the Church Fathers lend themselves to this misuse. Following the precedent set by the writer of the Gospel of John, they speculated that it was the masculine 'Logos' of God which united with the human substance (or essence) of the baby boy Jesus[2].

The Logos concept was a widespread and diffuse notion in the Ancient world. According to C.K.Barrett, 'Logos is a Greek word of many meanings, most of which can be summarized under the two heads of inward thought, and the outward expression of thought in speech. In a theistic system it could therefore naturally be used in an account of God's self-revelation: his thought was communicated by his speech.'[3] The early Stoic philosophers believed that the Logos was an impersonal 'World Soul', an ordering rational principle within the cosmos. Men could become sons of God by virtue of a divine spark, a fragmentary logos which dwelt within. Every rational human being possessed to a lesser or greater extent this 'spermatikoi logoi', literally sperm of the logos[4]. It is important to note here the masculine metaphor. In Greek thinking the reason or mind is masculine since it derives from the Absolute or God. Women were considered deficient in reasoning and moral powers and thus further in the chain of Being from the source of Reality.

By the beginning of the Christian era Stoic ethics and Platonic cosmology provided a broad philosphical paradigm for the Hellenistic world view. In this paradigm the Logos came to be understood in increasingly personal terms, as a divine intermediary being who communicated knowledge of God, creation and redemption to the human (read male) mind. In popular religiosity gods such as Hermes and Thoth were called Logos. Oscar Cullmann comments, 'The word Logos came to be used to give an allegorical, philosophical explanation to myths about the gods'[5]. If we ask what is the precise origin for the logos christology which is to be found in the Prologue to John's Gospel, there are according to Barrett two sources. The first is the thinking of the First Century Jewish philospher Philo of Alexandria.

He created a synthesis between the Stoic-Platonic Logos philosphy and Jewish biblical exegesis. Philo's Logos is the Archetypal Man who is not only the blueprint for the human race but also the rational principle of the universe who mediates the Mind of God to man through the Mosaic Law and allegorical figures such as the High Priest and Moses[6]. However, the closest parallel between the Johannine Logos and Hellenistic philosphical speculation is to be found in the 'Corpus Hermeticum'. This is a body of literature written down between the Second and Fourth Centuries but clearly incorporating Christian and gnostic beliefs from the First Century. Here a mediating Logos or Heavenly Man brings salvific knowledge from God to initiates who are divinely reborn and freed from the evil world for ultimate union with God[7].

Rosemary Ruether has argued that it was unnecessary for the Church Fathers to have used the Greek philosphical concept of the male Logos to 'explain' their doctrine of the incarnation. They could have used the Jewish reflections upon Wisdom. I agree with this observation for there was already in Jewish Hellenism and indeed in the Sapiental books of the Hebrew Bible an older tradition of speculation upon a divine mediator between God and humanity, namely 'Hokmah', or in Greek 'Sophia', the Wisdom of God. Sophia is described as the female hypostasis of God who is the creative, revelatory wisdom and justice of God. Jesus and Paul refer to her frequently[8] whereas the Logos is only referred to three times in the New Testament and only by the Johannine writer[9]. It is interesting to note that Philo of Alexandria and the writer of John's Gospel actually replaced Sophia with Logos, presumably under the influence of Hellenistic syncretism. Ruether's point is that if Sophia rather than the Logos had been incorporated into the doctrine of the incarnation then the sexist belief would never have evolved in Christian tradition that since Jesus was male and the Logos is male God must logically be ontologically male (that is in the essence of God's being[10]).

In this essay I wish to explore the possibility of rethinking incarnational christology so that it affirms the salvation and divinization of women. Not abstract 'Woman' as a category of philosophy but real embodied historical women in search of their own contemporary subjectivity. From the outset we need to realise what a fundamental shift in Christian theology such an approach requires. The Roman

Catholic defence of its male priesthood is based upon the argument that believers need to experience sacramental signs in the liturgy which correspond with the evangelical message of their faith. Since Jesus was male there should therefore be a physical resemblance between the priest and Christ. Behind this apparently innocuous and simple statement is a Thomist theological presupposition, namely that since there must be an analogy between the things of earth and the things of heaven, only men can represent Christ in the priestly mediatorial and sacrificial functions because Christ within the Godhead is male!

The Protestant churches have traditionally interpreted the Logos less metaphysically. Their starting point is that the creative and redemptive Word of God is revealed in the Bible and supremely in Jesus Christ. The minister of the Word was traditionally male because men are head of women just as Christ is head of the Church. The reasoning, (backed up by selective Pauline injunctions) that the Minister must be male because he represents the sovereign authority of Christ to his congregation has slowly been eroded during this century by a combination of better biblical exegesis, women's emancipation and a fundamental shift in thinking about the role of the pastor in the church. However belief that Jesus is the Son of God the Father and therefore God is male remains deepseated. It is reinforced by the androcentric language of the Bible and the fact that Jesus was male. Attempts to introduce inclusive language into the liturgy, hymns, prayers and Bible are still resisted vehemently on grounds which appear more emotional than theological.

In my opinion it is only possible to bring women into the centre of an incarnational christology if the traditional categories are gender reversible; if, in other words, we may speak of the Divine incarnated in a female body, 'truly God and truly female' or as the Dutch feminist theologian Anne-Claire Mulder argues, we may speak of the female flesh becoming Word/Logos[11]. If this proves to be impossible on Christian theological or moral grounds, then I must sadly conclude that Mary Daly was correct when she observed, 'If God is male then the male is God'[12] and 'Salvation comes only through the male'[13].

I shall begin this investigation by asking what exactly is incarnational christology and how did it evolve? If we can formulate a clearer definition of the doctrine we shall be in a better position to evaluate whether it can contribute to the search for female subjectivity.

85

The Paradox of the Chalcedon Dogma

At first sight it would appear that the Chalcedon dogma that Jesus was 'truly God and truly man' is both sexist and idolatrous. It is also not a coincidence that the dogma effectively silenced many heterodox theologians and recalcitrant religious movements. For example, after the Council of Chalcedon in 451 C.E. the Emperor issued an imperial edict that any army officer who opposed the dogma should be stripped of his rank. Congregations were also manipulated; during Holy Week 457 C.E. Proterius the patriarch of Alexandria was lynched by a pro-Chalcedon mob[14]. However it would be facile to explain away the dogma as a purely politically motivated piece of theological mumbo jumbo, or a product of male clerical or imperial hubris. There is at the heart of the dogma an extraordinary and radical belief, namely that the divine nature was united with, whilst remaining different from, the human nature of the Jewish prophet Jesus of Nazareth. In other words that the classical Greek dualism between divine spirit and human body had been transcended. God was incarnate in the flesh and in Christ humanity was incorporated into the being of God.

Since the 1960s many Western liberal theologians have rejected the doctrine of the incarnation as an illogical, irrelevant and unbiblical myth[15]. In her doctoral dissertation, 'The Redemption of God: A Theology of Mutual Relation', the feminist theologian, Carter Heyward also took this position. She wrote, 'Jesus matters only if he was fully, and only, human. Otherwise we are speaking of something/someone who bore no fully and only human relation to God or his sisters and brothers.'[16] Ten years later however, Heyward rejects her earlier view. She writes, 'But the pendulum swing toward Jesus of history is not necessarily an affirmation of humanity. It can serve as a means of perpetuating the notion of a deity who remains above human experience, a god who really is not involved with us. If, in emphasizing Jesus' humanness, we contend that Jesus was 'fully and only human' (as I myself wrote a decade ago), such a claim can be interpreted as a rejection of the reality or possibility of incarnation.'[17]

Heyward is faced with a paradox which haunts contemporary feminist christology, namely how is it possible to affirm the presence of God in the female embodied subject and yet bypass the Chalcedon dogma? The dogma is a conundrum. For on the one hand it affirms as an article of faith that the essential dualistic split between God as transcendent Subject and humanity as mortal object has been overcome. Since many feminist theologians regard androcentric theological dualism as the fundamental problem between the sexes the dogma appears to be a liberating step into a new kind of epistemology and subjectivity. However, as Heyward points out, the dogma is predicated upon dualism. If the Church Fathers had not diluted the Gospel with Stoic-Platonic dualism they would not have needed to spend six centuries conceptualising a hypostatic union and then disputing the exact relationship between the Logos, the human and divine ousia (nature) and the human and divine will within Jesus of Nazareth. In this sense I agree with Heyward that 'classical christology, as an area of constructive work, is dead'[18].

Heyward is tentatively searching for a new way of approaching incarnational christology based upon 'a praxis of relational particularity and co-operation'[19]. She writes, 'In this praxis theological knowledge would cease to be a matter of discerning the Christ and would become instead a matter of generating together images of what is redemptive or liberating in particular situations'[20]. Moments of collective confessional prophetic action and of fully embodied (sensual and erotic) connections in relation to one another, other creatures, and the earth are 'christic' revelations of the relation between Jesus of Nazareth, our stories and the Sacred[21].

It seems to me that Heyward has not fully rejected the Chalcedon formula. Rather she has rejected the authority of the dogma as the test of orthodoxy. She has begun to explore what incarnation as an experience of God rather than as a doctrine about the unicity of Christ might mean. In other words, by replacing the discrete name 'Christ' with the adjective 'christic' Heyward is claiming that the essence of the dogma is applicable to everyone engaged in the ethical and redemptive search for right-relation and liberation. The uniqueness and universality of Jesus Christ as Logos, Lord, Son of God, New Adam and Pantocrator (lord of the Universe) has been replaced by the uniqueness and universality of the christic experience. This experience could be described as the divinization of the embodied subject through passionate and justice-making relationships. God is the presence and power in and between these relationships.

I find Heyward's use of the adjective 'christic' and Brock's usage of Christa- community very thought provoking[22]. In the Pauline epistles 'Christ' is often used as a collective noun, the Church for example is described as the aggregate 'Body of Christ'. Further Paul used 'being in Christ' as an ethical-spiritual experience. Dennis Nineham has pointed out that the Chalcedon dogma was a response to Christian collective experience. He wrote, 'During and after the Arian controversy, when the full divinity of Christ was called into question, the reply was, in essence, that the Christians knew themselves to enjoy a condition- call it 'divinization' or what you will- which would have been impossible unless full divine ousia had been present in Jesus; therefore such full divinity must have been present in him.'[23] This observation correlates with the well known position of Athanasius and the Eastern tradition that God the Logos had become man so that men might become divine[24].

It would seem to be the case then that incarnational christology emerged as the theological reflection of the Church upon a salvific experience which was evoked through their devotion to Jesus and the God whom he revealed. It is not the case that Jesus spoke of himself as divine although as we have seen that he did claim to have knowledge of the Kingdom of God and he possessed prophetic and healing powers. The early Jewish Hellenistic Christians were monotheists who awaited the Eschaton and their final vindication in the name of their Lord Jesus and in the power of the Holy Spirit of God. The divinization of Jesus began as the Christian missionaries sought to give expression to their sense of salvation in the Greco-Roman world. In this milieu descending and ascending redeemer myths, the appearance of the gods in human, animal or phantom form, gnostic speculations concerning a Heavenly or Divine Man and emperor worship were the order of the day.

Frances Young has illustrated this religious milieu and the problems it raised for Christian apologetics vividly by examining the defence written by Origen against the pagan polemicist Celsus[25]. Celsus had two main criticisms of the Christian claim to the divinity of Jesus. Firstly he argued that Jesus was just one of many frauds wandering around Palestine claiming, 'I am God, or a son of God or a divine spirit'[26]. Origen's sole defence was that unlike Simon Magus or Dositheus Jesus had been successful in attracting large numbers of followers. Young comments, 'It was not a bad argument in the

88

syncretistic atmosphere of the Hellenistic world where faith was 'directed to divine power rather than divine personalities' (i.e. the believer cared more about the success-rate of a god or his prophet than the precise identity or character).'[27]

The main argument of Celsus was that unlike the epiphanies of Apollo and Asclepius who 'came down' with oracles and miracles, Jesus was born and died in the normal way and therefore could not have been a god. Origen replied by claiming that Jesus was born of a virgin like Plato whose mother Amphictione was visited by Apollo[28]. Origen is considered to be the first great Eastern Christian scholar. He developed the doctrine of the Logos and the virgin birth to give a theological form to his experience of Christian apotheosis, that is, of transcending his sinful mortal body through a mystical union with God in Christ. In his 'Contra Celsum' we can see the context of his thinking and experience. He lived in a world of descending and ascending lesser gods and semi-divine beings and he wished to try to show that Jesus was in a unique sense a revelation of the one true God in spite of the historical fact that his incarnation was fully in the human flesh and that he suffered and died. This was unthinkable in Greek philosophy since the God behind the gods of the myths was considered to be Absolute Being and as such, unchanging, unmoving, unfeeling and wholly transcendent beyond time and space.

I agree with Heyward that this religious milieu and the classical incarnational christology it engendered are now at best an anachronism. Modern western Christians do not share the ancients' pessimism towards the material and mortal world. The desire for apotheosis in the sense of escaping the physical prison of the body can be considered not only irresponsible but immoral. Rosemary Ruether for example, has argued that, 'Eschatological hope has been related to the alienation from and disappointment with bodily life and its processes of seasonal and generational renewal,...sexuality, maternity, the female body, became despised as the images of a sinful life whence comes death, that is merely mortal life'[29].

Ruether achnowledges that the creeds of Nicea and Chalcedon were formulated to try to overcome this world-denying body-spirit dualism. The Church Fathers attempted to counter the popular Gnostic view that creation was evil 'by saying that the liberating Messiah is also the Logos through which the world was created'[30] but in practice the Church was deeply ascetical and male/mind orientated. Augustine for example, not only believed that sin and mortality were passed from one generation to the other through sexual intercourse but he also claimed that the divine command to 'be fruitful and multiply' had been rescinded by God[31]. The Church Fathers regarded women as dangerous daughters of Eve whose very physical presence aroused fleshly temptations. Only initiated virgins or widows were allowed minor functions in the congregation. The male bishops and monks devoted themselves to the only pure female, the 'Theotokos', Mary the virgin Mother of God.

In my opinion, if modern western Christians wish to retain the central insight of the Chalcedon dogma that Jesus was 'truly God and truly man' then they need to radically reinterpet what this means. I hope that this essay has demonstrated that the dogma arose as a theological reflection upon the person of Jesus of Nazareth and the salvific experience of God that his life, death and resurrection engendered amongst early Christians; further that the form of the dogma was a response to a specific missionary context, namely the Hellenistic world with its syncretistic mixture of popular gods, high Stoic-Platonic philosophy and wide-spread disgust with the material and mortal world.

A new relevant incarnational christology can only emerge if the contemporary correlative conditions are taken into account. In other words the questions we need to address are; what is our understanding of Jesus of Nazareth and his relationship to God? What is our experience and hope of salvation and liberation? And what are the religious, philosophical and social contexts of our societies? Feminist theologians are faced with an additional question namely, how can the incarnation of God in the female flesh be integrated into christology? I shall restrict my answers here to a tentative exploration of two possible approaches to this last point. I shall not address the implicit presupposition that the divine and holy Being is incarnate in the female flesh because I, as a religious woman, experience this to be so.

'Truly God and Truly Female' – the Incarnation and the Female Subject

The simplest way to reintegrate women into incarnational christology is to reaffirm the humanity of Jesus. This is the position of many

American feminist theologians. For example, Letty Russell describes Jesus as first and foremost a new sort of Person. As the Christ he is the representative of the new redeemed humanity before God and is also 'God's re-presentation of the humanity of God'[32]. Women can live a 'journey into freedom' because God's actions in Christ have an 'overspill' in our ongoing struggle to become the subjects of our own history. Russell claims that in her view of christology, the maleness of Jesus is totally irrelevant. She writes, 'To think of Christ first in terms of his male sex or his racial origin is to revert again to a biological determinism which affirms that the most important thing about a person is her or his sex or colour.'[33] Rosemary Ruether holds a similar view; every individual in the human race has the divine potential to become part of 'redeemed humanity' irrespective of sex, race or class[34]. Elisabeth Fiorenza, as we have seen, develops a variation on this gender-equality-in- Christ approach. She emphasises the Jesus Movement as a new sort of social and historical subjectivity, the 'discipleship of equals' or 'the ecclesia of self-identified women and women-identified men'[35].

If one accepts that the differences between the sexes/genders is only a question of cultural and historical factors which can be remedied by full socio-economic and political equality between the sexes, then this appears a reasonable position to take. However, the problem with this approach is that it tends to reaffirm body-mind dualism. To speak of Christ or women and men abstractly as humanbeings is to create the illusion that people are sexually neutral and that their bodies do not matter. Ruether comes very close to this position in her discussion of male and female anthropology when she says, 'To put it bluntly, there is no biological connection between male gonads and the capacity to reason. Likewise, there is no biological connection between female sexual organs and the capacity to be intuitive, caring, or nurturing'[36]. Ruether denies that she is wishing to affirm androgyny, rather 'all humans possess a full and equivalent human nature and personhood, as male and female'[37]. In my opinion, if sexual difference is ignored or glossed over, such a statement simply begs the question what is a person?

The Church Fathers in spite of their grounding in neo-Platonic philosophy, realised that in order to affirm the reality of the incarnation of God in the flesh, it was necessary to stress the sex of Jesus. The humanity of God in Christ took a personal form through the human male Jesus of Nazareth. Thus the Chalcedon text begins, 'Following therefore the holy fathers, we confess one and the same our Lord Jesus Christ, and we teach harmoniously (that he is) the same perfect in godhead, the same perfect in manhood, truly God and truly man, the same of a reasonable soul and body; 'homoousios' (that is of the same substance/essence -JH) with the Father in godhead, and the same homoousios with us in manhood, like us in all things except sin...'[38].

In my opinion, if we wish to stress the particularity of the incarnation, in other words that during the historical life of a specific woman or man, God is present and active in the flesh, then we cannot avoid the issue of sexual difference. For the fundamental difference between the sexes is biological (emotions and feelings have an organic base). Other differences such as the socialisation of children into the genders masculine and feminine can be regarded as the attempt of a specific culture or religion to order the differences into a patriarchy. For example, the difference in power between the sexes is a cultural creation based upon male fear of the biological otherness of women and male desire to control female sexuality. In the Early Catholic Church taboos around female menstruation and giving birth led directly to the exclusion of women from the altar and thus to the ecclesiastical hierarchy of the Church. It follows that if we wish to affirm that God is incarnate in the female flesh then the Divine Presence should logically be located in the embodied female subject.

In spite of continued attempts by bishops and Church leaders to insist that the sexuality and fertility of women should be carefully controlled by man-made moralites and structures, I believe that many modern Christians have consciously rejected the taboo around sexuality and the female body. The causal link between sin and sex has been broken. The 'miracle of birth' and even the joys of erotic love are shared privately between parishoners even if there comes only a thundering silence from the pulpit. However the resistance to the use of female metaphors and images for God in the liturgy demonstrates that there remains a deep-seated fear and even loathing of the female dimension of God. Paul Tillich accounted for this in psychological terms. He has argued that God as the 'ground of being' is best symbolised in female terms. He wrote, 'In so far as it is symbolical, it points to the mother-quality of giving birth, carrying, and embracing, and, at the same time, of calling back, resisting independence of the created, and swallowing it.'[39] Tillich claimed Protestants are afraid of this dimension of God.

Tillich's 'explanation' is in my opinion very strange. Why does he associate the immanent being of God with a sort of claustrophobic ever-devouring Womb? Could it be that Tillich himself shares the view that he attempts to correct, namely that the male must assert his freedom and morality by breaking the mother-bond and ascending to the father God? Many theologians, philosphers, psychologists and cultural anthropologists have studied women as an object of difference in order to find themselves as a subject. When I stress the difference between the sexes as the starting point for a feminist incarnational christology I do not advocate that women simply turn the tables on men. Rather, one of the claims I would wish to assert is that women who know God and commune with God in themselves, in relationship with others and in relationship to the cosmos need not be afraid or ashamed to also search in their embodied experience for images and knowledge of the Divine. The objectification, denigration and even sometimes demonization of female biological processes and sexuality is a male problem. Women suffer from this male problem directly through experiences of incest, sexual abuse, pornography, rape and their exclusion from some holy orders. However, they do not need to internalise these male projections or passively accept violence against their bodies and minds. Rather they can reclaim their embodied selves as made in the image of God and potentially a source of divine presence. The meeting of the divine essence and the human essence in the female flesh can only take place if women can learn to love and cherish their own bodies.

A woman who knows that God is incarnate in the world in women as well as men has made an important step in her own liberation from the existential guilt of being born a daughter of Eve. But how is she to move from believing this as an abstract article of faith to feeling and knowing God in herself as a woman subject in her own right? This is difficult to realise because there are so few role-models of self-defined women. Historically, the majority of women were considered the possessions of their fathers, sons and husbands. They functioned as mothers, workers or nuns for men and within male-defined boundaries. Even exceptional women such as queens, abbesses, mystics and writers

93

were protected by powerful male sponsors who influenced their values, thoughts and behaviour. In other words whilst women in every generation and class have struggled often against all the odds to survive and bring up their children, one could say that women who consciously and publically defined their own identity and subjectivity on the basis of their own female experience were and are very few on the ground. Hopefully this shall change with female emancipation. However, it is important to keep in mind how new and fragile the emerging female subject in history really is. For example, the majority of European women have gained access to higher education, adequate health provision, and a political and economic say only after the Second World War.

For those women who have struggled in this century to gain entry into the man's world of culture, politics and the Christian Ministry, there has proved to be much frustration and disappointment. The agenda has been set by male tradition and practice, women are expected to either function as the pretty girl around the office or to somehow become surrogate men or sexless career machines. After thirty years of so-called women's emancipation, working women are faced with restricted room to manoeuvre in how they organise their work and child-care, influence policy-making or develop their skills. Much energy and ingenuity is diverted into thinking of strategies and tactics to survive with a modicum of integrity in the modern (male) work place. This workplace is basically a highly bureaucratic, market-orientated, high-tec. aggressive environment. The message to women workers is clear; adapt or admit that you are not emotionally suited for the modern Western economy and return to your proper place as the ideal homemaker, wife and mother

It is in this context of the reality of work, that feminists are beginning to realise that the old agenda of sexual equality through equal opportunity does not address the heart of the matter. There are in fact fundamental differences between the sexes based upon a complex interaction between biology (sex) and socialisation (gender). Women think, feel, make moral decisions, act, communicate and organise differently from men. The challenge is to find the source of these differences: to be able to ascertain which belong to women in their own right and can be used for a liberating identity and which are created by the male images of women in the dominant culture.

94

The discussion around sexual difference began in France with the writings of the feminist philosopher Simone De Beauvoir. Her well known comment, 'One is not born a woman, one becomes one'[40] was a critique of the construction of the feminine by male writers, philosophers and theologians. It is not suprising given the legacy of De Beauvoir that French feminism in particular has concerned itself with the deconstruction of male texts, the so-called 'écritures des femmes'[41]. Their project is part of a broader stream in French critical culture which is called post-structuralism in Europe and post-modernism in America and Britain. This disparate movement and philosophy began in France in the late 1960's with the work of philosphers such as Michel Foucault and Jacques Derrida. Post-modernism is not a coherent systematic philosphy but rather a critique of modernism, that is the thinking and presuppositions of the European Enlightenment which still dominate our education system and political and economic structures and policies. Post-modernism rejects the belief of the Cartesian male that he is a free, autonomous and moral thinking subject. According to Derrida the subject is as much a text written by language and culture as he is a man of reason who can independently think his way to the truth or reality. All truth is mediated through thought and all thought is created by language which comes from society and culture not from the individual[42].

In the context of this discussion it is interesting to see how Lacan, the so-called 'French Freud', adapted post-modernism for his psychoanalytic theory and clinical practice. For Lacan took over Derrida's critique of western discourse as 'logocentric' and gave it a psychoanalytical interpretation. For Lacan, thought is the forming in words of basic desires within the unconscious. He maintained that we think in logocentric language because the symbolic ordering of our unconscious has been created through the imprinting of a cultural 'law', the 'rule of the Father'[43]. According to Lacan, from the moment a girl child is born she hears only a language created by a male culture to enforce the power of fathers/God the Father. To become a woman (read 'for men'- JH), the girl needs to overcome her physical-emotional resistance to the Logos through the stages leading up to and culminating in the Oedipus Complex where her desire is finally fully channelled towards her father. The French psychoanalyst and feminist philospher Luce Irigaray studied under Lacan but was finally expelled

95

from his École Freudienne' because she took her teacher's clinical observations to their logical conclusion. Namely if the female sex is simply a sign of the 'feminine' which men (and by implication women) lack, then the female as subject does not exist[44]. Women themselves must then begin to create a new language and culture based upon a positive affirmation of their embodied existence and desires.

In my opinion it is not a coincidence that Derrida chose the symbol Logos to describe the essence of western discourse or that Irigaray is exploring Christian christology and incarnational thinking[45]. There is a certain convergence between the post-modernist and the feminist theological critique of modern male epistemology since both movements are concerned to show how the binary either-or European discourse of rationalism functions ideologically to sustain the power of elite male groups in culture and society. However whilst male post-modernism has the tendency to relativise reality to the point of nonsense or absence of meaning feminists have a clear and practical goal for deconstruction. Namely, that through critically analysing speech, texts and symbols, women begin to develop a language and process of thinking and feeling based upon their own self-defined identity as women. The Dutch feminist theologian Anne-Claire Mulder believes that Irigaray's project, which seeks to create a female symbolic order based upon the specific form of the female body and the specific female desire of 'jouissance' (erotic love of Life) can be described as the female flesh becoming Logos. Women creating their own embodied language and discourse are simultaneously creating an identity as a self-defined 'I' and bridging the classical dualism between body and soul, emotion and reason, God as immanent and God as transcendent[46].

In my opinion the struggle of women for equal rights in the political and socio-economic sphere and the existential quest of women to become the subjects of their own bodies/selves are both essential aspects of women's liberation. These twin projects of external collective action and internal personal mysticism need to be developed simultaneously. However in terms of a feminist incarnational christology I should now choose to emphasise the becoming of God in the female flesh rather than the presence of God in the abstract human being. The locus for the life-giving and redemptive power of God in the flesh must include the sexually embodied reality of a person's historical and religious life.

I doubt that when bishop Athanasias claimed that 'God became man so that men might become divine' he was referring to the female embodied-self, rather his incarnational christology was directed to the male mind-soul. The difference does appear fundamental. If the difference is anything more than biology only time will tell. For the present, women who are searching for divinization in their physical-thinking-becoming sense of self and in their daily work and lives have chosen a difficult and narrow path which requires integrity, courage and communion with the Wisdom of God. A Christian woman can take heart that this Wisdom is a promise and grace of God because in the life, death and resurrection of Jesus of Nazareth she can catch a glimpse of the presence of Wisdom in the male flesh. Her experience as a woman is different from that of Jesus but because she bears the Divine Presence in her own body she understands that the wounds of love and the thirst for justice can transcend the differences between women and men, women and God.

CONCLUDING CHRISTOLOGICAL REFLECTIONS

'The Kingdom of Heaven is within you'[1]

In this concluding chapter I wish to try and draw the strands of my christological reflections together. Further, I wish to tease out the implications of these essays for a contemporary understanding of ecclesiology, spirituality and ethics. However before I begin, I feel that it is necessary to make some futher comments about our European context. For that context has radically altered during the four years that I have been writing this book. The speed of change raises fundamental questions concerning the method of building a christology 'from below', that is from out of the experience of faith-communities. For example, to speak of 'European women' four year ago meant for me to reflect upon the emergence of feminism within the context of Western European women's struggle for equal rights, obligations and a voice in education, research and theology. The women theologians and ministers I met from Eastern Europe through the 'European Society of Women in Theological Research' were a small group whose main concern was the survival of their confessional churches within state communism.

Today women from many Eastern European countries such as Hungary, Poland, East Germany, the Czech Republic, Estonia, Latvia, Lithuania and Rumania are seeking to play a full part in the shaping of European theology. Their attitudes and beliefs are a challenge to Western philosophical, theological and political presuppositions. For example, the Czech feminist theologian Jana Opocenska in dialogue with Mary Grey has argued, 'It may be useful to realize clearly that our civilization has reached its bottom. The shaking foundations of the European humanistic ideas are characteristic of the 20th century. If 9 children out of 12 have to die, if 50,000 people die daily because of famine, then we all live in a strange chaos.'[2] Opocenska then went on to cite with approval the view of Eric Hobsbawm, 'At the global level, the 21st century will have to face at least three problems which are getting worse: the growing gap between the rich world and the poor (and probably between the rich and poor within the rich world); the rise of racism and xenophobia; and the ecological crisis which effects us all. The ways in which they can be dealt with are unclear, but privatization and the free market are not among them.'[3]

Opocenska and other Eastern European women do not regard the collapse of state socialism as a victory for Western capitalism but rather as a tragic failure of the socialist ideal. They feel keenly that market economics, individualism and secularization breed social injustice and dangerous forms of nationalism and racism. Considering the rapid growth of neo-nazism in Germany, the European recession, the collapse of the Italian political system under the weight of corruption and the vicious civil war in the disintegrated Yugoslavia, all events which have happened since the pulling down of the Berlin Wall, one can sympathise with their fears. The ideological vacuum in Europe cannot be shored up with stocks and shares.

Rapid Change and Fluid Identitity in Europe

Reflecting upon these events and the continuing efforts of Europeans to create a United European Union, I have come to understand the European identity as something extremely fluid and characterised by difference and discontinuity. Europe is not defined by clear geographical boundaries, frontiers are continually changing. Nor do we all share the same Christian tradition. The differences between Protestant north, Roman Catholic south and Orthodox east do seem fundamental. Further our European cultural heritage is not uniform. The great European historical epochs such as the Holy Roman Empire, the High Middle Ages, the Renaissance, the rise of Early Capitalism, the Enlightenment, the Industrial Revolution and emergence of modern European democracies occurred at a different pace and form in different lands. Even the national differences between Europeans are not simply to be defined in terms of race or geographical boundaries. They have also been shaped by complex factors such as migration, war and occupation, political and socio-economic developments, trading and colonial

99

history, art, music, philosophy and science. These characteristics constantly evolved and changed through interaction with neighbouring countries.

The rapidity of change and the fluidity of identity are in my opinion the two hallmarks of continental Europe. (The four nations of the British Isles and Ireland whilst protected by the sea from the continent have amply demonstrated these characteristics internally and in relation to each other). Does this mean that a contextual European christology should also be characterised by change and fluidity? Surely Christian faith at least can offer one steadfast rock in the sea of uncertainty? I think this a natural longing of all religious persons. We desire some sense of certainty and security in this 'vale of tears'. However there is a difference between trust in a steadfast God and doctrinal normativity. The former is an act of faith but the latter is an attempt to co-opt God through abstract propositions. The history of European christology is a history of attempts of particular confessions, races and theological schools to claim the normative higher ground about Jesus as the Christ. This is to a certain extent inevitable given the conflicting and changing interests of Europeans in relation to each other and the world at large. However, the speed of contemporary developments in Europe now makes it essential that we consciously recognise this process. That we accept that christology is contextual to specific groups. Only then can an honest and respectful ecumenical dialogue take place.

The question still remains how much change and fluidity should we accept in a contemporary christology? Change for changes sake should hardly be the criterion for a modern spirituality and ethics! In my opinion we need to search for qualitative change. We know that organic change is essential to life. Without constant change life processes should atrophy and die. But we also know that healthy growth follows the law of the nature of the organism. Mutant and accelerated change lead to sicknesses such as cancer. The search for a spirituality and ethics in a world of change is a pilgrimage into the depths of Life. We seek the internal laws governing processes of renewing change and interaction and we try to flow with this life-giving current of God-with-us. Christology then may change with new experiences and depths of insight about the world and God. The test for a contemporary christology in a time of change is how far new understandings and images of Jesus empower us to seek in the depths

100

of the present the qualities and values necessary for the healing and renewing of ourselves, our societies and our planet. A christology without some kind of eschatological or utopian dimension of hope has in my opinion sold out to secularisation.

Fluidity of identity is for Europeans perhaps more destabilising than change. Afterall change in the sense of progress and development is a classic myth of European liberalism. But how do I cope with the different identities of modern Europe? Once I was a simple English woman, now I must learn to adapt to a dual citizenship as English and European. This Europe has many interests and voices. Through the media, information technology and international marketing comes a cacophony of voices with competing claims, scientific theories, slogans and advertisements. Anyone who can pay the price can claim my attention and I must be sympathetic and yet suspicious in order to separate the sheep from the goats.

But it is not only the rich, powerful and charismatic who speak in the many voices of Europe. Oppressed and ignored groups are becoming articulate and demanding recognition and the right to create their own agendas and research their own histories. In order to contribute honestly and justly to European life I need therefore to respect the specific differences of 'the other'. For as the Jewish philosopher E.Levinas has shown, the Western humanist tradition which has given priority to the synthesizing and harmonizing of Europeans has led to intolerance and denial of difference[4]. In her dissertation, the Dutch feminist ethicist Annelies van Heijst develops the thinking of Levinas in terms of an ethic of 'difference-in-relation. She challenges feminists to think carefully about their efforts for self-determination. Are we becoming so self-assertive that we are in danger of losing the ability to risk our own power and position in order to listen to the stranger's voice? For it is precisely the strangeness of 'the other' which constantly challenges our presuppositions and therefore creates the possibility of new interpretations of oneself and the world, moral choices and political decisions[5].

The many voices of Europe speak in different languages. Once I thought in one language and assumed that my thoughts were my own, that I created my ideas ex nihilo. Now that I speak in several languages I have come to realise that to a great extent languages and therefore ideas are the creations of specific cultures and the patriarchal symbolic order. The English language had shaped and bounded my thoughts. Now my ideas are becoming as fluid as my cultural identity.

The growing sense of the fluidity of personal and national identity within Europe could lead to dangerous identity confusion or to a renewed anthropology, psychology and philosophy. It is unclear at this juncture in time which direction Europeans will choose. We do seem to be at a point of cultural crisis. However since living in the Netherlands I have begun to see signs of an emerging new consciousness. It is interesting to observe, for example, how quickly feminism has adapted to this situation. Whereas in the 1960s and 70s the Women's Movement emphasised the old liberal humanist agenda of the struggle for emancipation through a collective appeal to equality there has been a marked shift of emphasis in the 1980s and 90s. The harmony model ('we are all sisters together!') has given way to networks of different voices and interest groups as women began to realise that race, culture, religion, socio-economic status and sexual preference make a fundamental difference to what one means by equal rights and opportunities. These networks of differing but interacting forms of feminism have made the Women's Movement less homogenous but has given her the flexibility and openness to constantly adapt, improve her research and theory-forming and create space for internal criticism and experimentation. Fluidity of identity for feminism has meant rejecting artificial structures of unity in favour of an ever-changing and transforming process of dialogue, interaction and creativity. The identity of feminism in Europe is no longer a set of fixed theories, political goals or structures but an open-ended process of women seeking a new sort of subjectivity where autonomy and relationality are both vital components[4].

The Italian feminist philosopher Rosi Braidotti has posed the question to European feminist theologians as to how far we are prepared to accept 'the differences within' ourselves which is so much part of 'secular' continental feminist thinking around sexual difference[5]. She argues, 'Identity for me is a play of multiple, fractured aspects of the self; it is relational, in that it requires a bond to the 'other'; it is retrospective, in that it is fixed through memories and recollections, in a genealogical process. Last, but not least, identity is made up of successive identifications, that is to say unconscious internalized images which escape rational control. This fundamental non-coincidence of identity with consciousness implies also that one entertains an imaginary relationship to one's history, genealogy and material conditions'[6]. Braidotti's point is that once feminists come to terms with how much complexity and multiplicity exists within their unconscious desires, even their desires for female subjectivity, they can learn to tolerate the contradictions, discontinuities, confusions and uncertainties within themselves, the political Women's Movement and society at large[7]. If women are to avoid dogmatic moralism and the European habit of scapegoating 'the other' whilst seeking to free themselves from the cultural constructions of 'the Woman' then they need to learn to accept their own shadowy and fragmented unconscious voices.

If one accepts the value of the emerging European feminist consciousness then the consequences for contemporary christology are far-reaching. Christology becomes not only contextual but also multifaceted. The discourse, beliefs, images, metaphors, symbols, spiritual practices and rituals around Jesus as the Christ will be shaped and given content differently by different faith-communites within the Ecumene of European faith-communities. Personally I do not find this a frightening prospect; it accords with the feminist understanding of the relation between truth and women's experience. For example Dale Spender writes, 'Outside a patriarchal framework there is no reason why theory cannot be formulated communally, the production of every woman having her say, and of having that say incorporated, so that theory is developmental....The process of explaining the world in all its diversity, interconnectedness and mulitiplicity of constructed meanings is not a substitute for theory but another form of theory'[8].

Spender is making a plea for a shift in the epistemological paradigm. In her opinion the rationalistic 'either-or' logic of Western thought and politics needs to give way to a multi-faceted, open ended 'both-and' discourse which recognises and values sexual and other differences. Truth is best grasped by the weaving together of diverse experience and praxis through a process of dialogue. Two fundamental criticisms have been levelled at this sort of theory of knowledge. Ethicists have asked how normative ethical principles can be deduced from such a relativistic approach to truth. I would argue that Spender is not describing the content of truth here but the process of sharing truth. That process is one of listening honestly and with respect to the other and then through discussion, criticism and evaluation finally reaching a temporary consensus and acting upon it until new experience requiring new criteria engenders further dialogue. This is surely how the United Nations functions practically in the field of human rights. If Christians could learn to relativise their truth claims and show more respect for each other's beliefs, many of the problems around the interpretation of Scripture and christology would cease to be emotional impediments to consolidated action in the face of the needs and suffering of the world.

A second criticism of a 'both-and' understanding of knowledge is doctrinal. Christians claim that the Bible and its witness to Jesus the Christ is divine revelation. Such truth is received through grace not constructed out of human experience. However there are different Christian understandings as to the nature of biblical revelation. The question is how God discloses God-self through Word, history and the Church. There are fundamentalist and evangelical Christians who claim to know 'Bible Truths' which they contrast zealously to 'fleshly' or 'materialistic' thinking. I cannot accept this sort of understanding of revelation as inerrent verbal inspiration because it idolises the Bible. The Bible and not the living, communicating, present God becomes the focus of faith. Further Christianity becomes an attempt to return to a mythical golden age rather than an engagement with the contemporary realities where God lives and moves and has being.

In my opinion the Bible is an ancient set of Holy Scriptures which cannot be interpreted justly without a knowledge of the historical contexts and original languages in which it was written. Further, whether Christians are conscious of it or not every encounter with the Bible involves a process of interpretation based upon contemporary human experience, for how can we read without language which is shaped by our culture and faith-communites? In this sense I agree with Rosemary Radford Ruether that, 'What have been called the objective sources of theology; Scripture and tradition, are themselves codified collective human experience. Human experience is the starting point and the ending point of the hermeneutical circle. Codified tradition both reaches back to roots in experience and is constantly renewed or discarded through the test of experience.'[9]

In her book, *The Wisdom of Fools? Seeking Revelation for Today* Mary Grey explores the possibility of using 'connectedness' as a new metaphor for Christian revelation[10]. She argues, 'Re-connecting -

104

earlier I called this 'redeeming the connections'- claims to be divine, because it is re-rooting in the basic relational energy of the universe. It is how we recover our energy and creativity, for our present situation, in contact with sustaining and nurturing memories from the past.'[11] In Grey's opinion the Western logos based 'either-or' rationalism is predicated upon a separate self and the denial of relation and as such has become a form of 'epistemic control' which has led to an inability in the West to listen to 'the other' with genuine openness and vulnerability. For her, the development of 'connected thinking' and the sensibility to be able to discern the communication of the divine are two aspects of the same project with far-reaching social and poltical consequences. She writes, 'If we are in fact a civilization of many overlapping discourses, the 'word' invites different cultural interpretations. For example, the concepts of 'freedom' and 'liberation' before, during and after communism and capitalism still struggle for 'authentic' interpretation and realization. Thus the key question now is, whether we are prepared to give attention to the silences, gaps and discontinuities in the proclamation of the Word. Are we prepared to ask awkward questions as to whose voice is excluded from official discourse? We would hope then for a Church able to respond in terms of a listening metanoia, a developing consciousness of the link between word and power.'[12]

The work of Mary Grey in the area of Christian redemption and revelation is an excellent example of how a feminist theologian can reflect upon contemporary experience and debates and add a profound spiritual and ethical dimension to the question of Western and in particular European identity. In opening herself to the many voices and discourses of Europe and European feminism Grey has found the resources to develop a profoundly relational theology. It is my hope that in the reconstruction of christology the same method 'from below' will be developed however intellectually or doctrinally 'risky' that appears to be. It is interesting to note here how Mary Grey's theology of connectedness leads towards a certain interpretation of Jesus. she writes, 'I am increasingly convinced that the meaning of incarnation is so profound that we willfully restrict it by seeing it totally encapsulated in the story of Jesus of Nazareth. What is revealed is relational power, the power of connection, which is of its essence not the private possession of an individual- as Jesus was well aware.'[13].

Christology 'From Below'

My essays are an attempt to approach christology 'from below'. This means two things, firstly that I have tried to begin with contemporary experience, particulary Christian-feminist spirituality and ethics. However flawed this deductive method may be, I am convinced that the Christian faith shall only be relevant if it listens to the pain, hopes and longings for salvation of those seeking God. Contemporary women in particular cannot be expected to coerce their growing sense of historical subjectivity into a doctrinal framework in which their experience has been ignored or silenced. A second meaning of christology 'from below' is the choice to concentrate upon the life of Jesus of Nazareth as represented in the writings of the earliest Christian communities rather than the doctrines surrounding the Christ. I am well aware that many biblical historians and theologians will regard this approach as naive. New Testament scholars are producing new and controversial research about Jesus at an unprecendented rate. Each year a new batch of large volumes is published[14]. The results fuel further debate and research and so the new quest for the historical Jesus continues with unabated momentum. It would be quite impossible to synthesise and integrate all this material into a christology 'from below'. Further this is not the intention of historical scholarship, rather scholars are engaged in a scientific discipline with its own discourse, criteria and schools of method and interpretation.

However whilst accepting and admiring this scholarly enterprise I am concerned that modern Christians and seekers of spiritual depth have been alienated from general knowledge about Jesus of Nazareth. Since many women have rejected the classical doctrinal tradition as a sexist symbolic order it is essential that they can read the Gospels afresh with a modicum of understanding of the historical contexts and theological presuppositions of the original writing communities. Otherwise it becomes quite impossible to enter into an honest dialogue with the Jesus Movement. If for example, the sense of eschatological crisis and hope is not understood, the phrases 'Kingdom of God', 'the time is at hand', 'believe the gospel' and 'Son of Man' become devoid of meaning and therefore relevance.

It has therefore been my intention to describe the broad parameters of our historical knowledge concerning Jesus of Nazareth and the earliest Christian communities. The technical details are fascinating for scholars but in my opinion not necessary for a christology 'from below'. What is necessary is that modern women have enough information to be able to read the Gospels without completely projecting their own presuppositions, values and norms onto the text. The christology which will emerge is their own spiritual and ethical dialogue and as I have shown will have particular and contextual features. I do not regard this as anarchistic. Theologians have always worked so. It is time that women become their own theologians!

A systematic theologian will find my approach naive for another reason. I have circumnavigated hundreds of years of doctrinal tradition as if the developmental nature of Church history had no relevance. I do accept that these short essays cannot do justice to the subtle changes and nuances of the history of Christian tradition. However in my defence I would argue, that in practice, not every part of that history is of equal relevance for our contemporary theologizing. In general, theologians have always tended to react upon the thinking of their closest historical predecessors. The controversies of the Church Fathers or Reformation and Counter-Reformation theologians are good examples of this tendency.

Living as an English Baptist in the Calvinist part of the Netherlands has made me aware how selective different confessions are in their use of christological traditions. For example, my colleague systematic theologians at the Gereformeerde Free University of Amsterdam build their christology particularly around certain Pauline texts as interpreted by Jean Calvin, the Dutch Calvinist School and the writings of Karl Barth. Calvin had a practical functionalist Christology, Christ has three Offices in the Church as Prophet, Priest and King[15]. The divinity of the Person of Christ scarcely plays a role in this biblical discourse. Rather the emphasis is upon the shared humanity of Christ and Christians, for according to the Dutch Reformed 'Confession of Faith' a Christian is a member of Christ anointed by the Spirit of God to share the same three Offices through her or his faith, sacrifice and authority[16].

From the perspective of the Nicean Creed, Calvinism is technically open to the charge of the 'heresy' of modalism, that is the belief that God is One and reveals Gods-Self in three modes as Creator, Saviour and Paraclete. But the term 'heresy' assumes that there is one Western christological tradition which is clearly not the case. The Dutch Reformed tradition has developed its own understanding of Jesus the Christ, which in every generation is criticised, reformulated and renewed according to the internal criteria of Dutch Reformed faith and practice. Considering Dutch moralism, the Reformed christological tradition is suprisingly open, flexible and innovative. For example, in the work of H.Berkhof (a leading contemporary theologian), the christology borders on 'adoptionism'. (That is the belief that God chose the obedient prophet Jesus to be a special son and thus infused him with the Holy Spirit. In other words, Jesus became gradually divinized through the actions of God his 'heavenly Father'[17].)

In contrast to the pragmatic and biblical language of Dutch Calvinism, I recently attended a conference on the theme of christology organised by the *English Society of the Study of Theology*[18]. Here I was confronted by a completely different kind of christological discourse which is prevalent in certain High Anglican, Roman Catholic and German Lutheran traditions of theology. This discourse is ontological and based upon 'trinitarian logic'. Thus there is a doctrinal appeal to the Cappadocian Fathers and the Council of Nicea. For example, Christoph Schwöbel argued that the Cappadocians initiated a revolution in ontology which makes it possible for contemporary Christians to understand relationality as essential to the Being of God. He argued, 'Locating the question of the divinity of Christ in the description of the relationship of the Father to the Son through the Spirit and of the Son through the Spirit to the Father brings a radical change to the understanding of the divinity of Christ. Christ is not divine because he possess a divine nature, but because God the Father relates to him in the Spirit as the Son and thereby distinguishes himself as the Father from the Son and in this way is in personal communion with the Son in the Spirit. Conversely, Christ is divine in relating to God the Father in the Spirit and thereby distinguishes himself as the Son from the Father and in this way is in personal communion with the Father and the Spirit.'[19]

Whilst the search for a relational and dynamic understanding of the nature of God is to be welcomed, christological discourse conducted exclusively in masculine language is offensive to many women. Their relationships as mothers, daughters, lovers and friends is shut out of the inner circle of relationality within the 'immanence' of the

108

Godhead[20]. The symbolic order of patriarchal relations is encapsulated in the symbolic order of God-talk. If Christian theology is to reach a point beyond the crisis of the feminist deconstruction of christology then the problem of such discourse for women has to be recognised as a fundamental issue. I hope that we can find a way forward. Male theologians can play their part in the search for a renewed ecumenical christology by taking the problem seriously. For example, women church historians and systematic theologians are beginning to conduct a scholarly re-evaluation of the Western tradition using new methods of research and interpretation. Their work is in some European universities and seminaries trivialised or suppressed. If theologians and churches continue to assume that their discourse is the only possible universally true means of expressing reality then they shall not only have failed to understand their own restricted contextual grasp of the Christian tradition but they shall also exacerbate the christological crisis.

Women searching for their own christological discourse will wish to go beyond the effort to deconstruct the tradition. A christology based solely upon criticism of the 'other' (here meaning the dominant masculine tradition) would be a negative and sexist way forward. A positive and inspiring christology needs to emerge from the traditions and resources of women of faith. European women have in fact a rich heritage upon which to draw. Womens' Studies is providing us with an extraordinary abundance of hitherto forgotten or ignored female creativity in the areas of literature, poetry, music, art, sciences, social and church history. Further, whilst it may be true that the patriarchal assignment of women to the private sphere of household work and family has shaped the lives of countless earlier generations of European women, it would be absurd to assume that women simply sat passively at home. In practice they developed emotional and social strategies to develop their gifts and insights. In particular they attuned themselves to the spheres of nature, bodily processes and the soul/psychology[21]. Thus women have had a hidden sub-culture or counter-culture within European spirituality, for example in the realms of mysticism, healing practices, piety, rituals and symbolic actions. The witch-hunts were attempts by the ecclesiastical and secular 'princes' to suppress this female spiritual and social power by labelling it demonic and eradicating its most potent practicioners.[22]

Intuitive Spirituality and Modern christologies

Many of the problems surrounding a contemporary faith concerning Jesus as Christ are in my opinion the product of Western dualistic theological presuppositions. For example, the concept of an almighty God the Father who is wholly transcendent (that is beyond time, space, change and feeling) leads to christological conundrums. Theologians need to engage in ingenious speculation to account for the incarnation, the crucifixion, the resurrection and the efficacy of the sacraments. This speculation has been conducted in the classical christological tradition in the language of metaphysics, in particular in terms of trinitarian categories. For contemporary Christians the language is not only mysterious but also incomprehensible. Most church-goers have pragmatically solved the riddle by committing the modalist 'heresy'. They pray to the Father, in the name of Jesus through the Holy Spirit as an act of faith in one God who reveals Gods-Self in three functions. The Father in popular Christian spirituality is the Creator and Judge, the Son is Jesus who as their Saviour and Friend reveals the way to God, and the Holy Spirit is the blessings of grace and virtue that God bestows. In other words, in my opinion most Christians are mono-theists. One is struck by how often 'ordinary' Christians in dialogue with their Hindu, Muslim or Jewish neighbours stress that 'we really all believe in the same God'.

Do we all believe in the same God? Is there one 'Ultimate Reality' behind all our religions as John Hick argues?[23] I believe this to be the case. However I would immediately wish to clarify what I mean. If there is one God then this God is not only the transcendent creator, sustainer and transformer of all cosmic, organic and historical processes, this God is also intimately involved as the loving Ground and matrix of Life. In other words God is present, immanent and communicative within our contemporary world and societies. I believe that many people have a religious sensibility, they are aware of ultimacy and depth within their lives and nature. They are also searching for signs of transcendence, intimations of a deeper significance to their daily lives, disclosures of a higher Reality. The challenge for Christian theology is to address the experience of these 'secular' people. Most modern Europeans simply do not find the Church as an institution attractive. Traditionalism does not speak to the reality of their lives in the modern world and fervent evangelicalism is exclusivistic, moralistic and centred upon a triumphalistic 'Jesus is Lord' christology.

For the many women Christians who have consciously chosen to leave the Church the reasons are more complex and painful. Rosemary Radford Ruether for example, speaks for many feminist Christians when she claims that women do not have to belong to a sexist Christian institution, rather they may claim the right to 'redefine the boundaries and the content of what it means to be the Church'[24]. Ruether speaks of 'women-church' as the exodus of women both within and beyond the ecclesia of patriarchy.

The reconstruction of a christology which can be interpreted as 'Good News' for alienated religious believers is in my opinion best served by avoiding metaphysical categories and atonement theories. Rather the Gospel is an invitation to join a pilgrimage of 'unknowing' into the living heart of God[25]. We need to focus our attention upon the transformative yet vulnerable presence of the loving God. If our spirituality is deep enough to embrace all aspects of life, whether personal, social, natural or cosmic then the theological controversies surrounding the nature of 'Christ' can respectfully be circumvented. Our focus becomes the God who reveals Gods-self as incarnate in different persons and history, who shares the suffering of the world and who is finally the creative power which continually transforms death into new life.

These aspects of the nature and processes of God-with-us are for Christians revealed in the simple story of the life, mission, death and resurrection of their Teacher, Jesus of Nazareth. If we can read the Gospels with some sense of historical perspective we can study these aspects for ourselves. We can learn to reflect, question, pray and act in the Spirit of the One God. It may well be that women studying the Gospels together are not actually interested in the debate concerning the nature of the relationship between the humanity and divinity of Christ within the Trinity. I suspect that they wish to search for a different way of knowing beyond the binary oppositional categories of Humanity versus Divinity, The World versus Eternity, the Secular versus the Sacred, the Body versus the Soul and the Individual versus Society. If this is the case then the christological issue for contemporary women is in fact a practical point concerning Christian authority. Women wish to be given the respect and space to use their own judgements, creativity and intuitions of the divine in their approach to the story of Jesus. Why do they have to conform to an androcentric and patriarchal doctrinal agenda in order to be Christians? In other words who has the authority to define and shape be-ing the Church?

There are Post-Christian feminist theologians such as Mary Daly and Daphne Hampson who have argued that christology is irredeemable for women[26]. Whilst I find their judgement too harsh I do sympathize with their position. If finally women are nor respected in their exodus journey beyond the Father-Son-(male)Holy Spirit symbolic order towards a spirituality and christology which comports with their intuitions of God and their quest for female subjectivity then the Church has failed in its mission to proclaim the Gospel of Jesus.

Eschatological Ethics

An important reason why I cannot accept the Post-Christian position is my understanding of religious ethics. There does seem to me to be a fundamental difference between the process by which public morality is reached by political debate and consensus and a religious ethic which has emerged through generations of contemplation upon the relationship between God and the created world. In the practice of morality both normative and religious ethics can be abused and perverted. My point is not that religious ethics are superior to the democratic process of normalizing certain values and behaviour but it is rather that religious reflection offers a depth of perspective and a different set of criteria which are necessary to approach the whole relational world ethically. Therefore I cannot agree with Daphne Hampson that Christianity is simply an unethical 'sexist myth'[27]. Reflection upon the life, actions, death and resurrection of Jesus of Nazareth is profoundly ethical because it challenges feminism and all other political movements to continual internal critique.

The story of how a good prophet who proclaimed that God is a loving, destabilizing force for human wholeness and justice came to be crucified as a blasphemer and state criminal is a shocking reminder of the tragic and alienated dimension of human power relations. This story formed the core of a new religion because people recognised it as a paradigm of the human condition. We all wish to be good people, ethical prophets and political reformers, we all wish to claim the higher moral ground. But are we prepared to pay the price? Do we wish to be misunderstood, misrepresented, persecuted, deserted and betrayed by our friends, tortured and martyred for our cause? Most of us do not so we try to flow with the consensus and gradually gain power through manipulation and exploitation of the 'other'. We consciously or unconsciously hang up these 'others' on the crosses of the world, whether they be 'the lazy unemployed', 'unmarried mothers', 'the immigrants' or the AIDS sufferer 'who brought it upon himself'.

The early Christians believed that those who forcefully seek religious, moral or political domination and control finally crucify God with their victims. This is a shocking myth which stands as an ethical judgement upon every endeavour to mould the world into our own image through force. The implications for our conduct of politics and economics in 'fortress Europe' and the world at large are farreaching. But also all forms of technology which tamper with the ecological balances of our planet stand under judgement. The eschatological ethics of the Jesus Movement are far more radical and incisive than we could formulate as a programme for equality between the sexes. Every aspect of discrimination, exploitation and abuse of power is exposed as destructive to the holiness and goal of Life.

Women seeking a religious ethic to deepen and objectify their own morality can theoretically choose from any religious tradition. Those who choose Christianity or who feel that they have no choice because for better or worse they are part of the Church have resources in the story of Jesus which can strengthen and inspire them in their quest for existential and historical subjectivity. If we believe that Jesus spoke under the Spirit of God when he claimed that God notices the sparrow that falls from her nest and that his healing ministry continues in every cup of water that we share, then our quest for Life in all its fullness is not a god-forsaken wandering in the wilderness. Whatever happens to us as we seek to live with courage and integrity we have a religious hope which roots us to the fertile Ground of Holy Life. Jesus said that we do not have to carry alone the anxieties and heavy burdens of daily life. The One who revealed that the religious hubris and political corruption of the demonic powers leads only to emptiness and who promised a Springtime when the broken hearts and bodies shall be transformed into new life, is within us.

113

NOTES

Chapter 1 / European Women and the Christological Crisis

1. Jesus to the Caananite woman, Matthew 15 v.28.
2. For an excellent overview of the history of European feminist theology see Catharina Halkes, 'Towards a History of Feminist Theology in Europe' in *Feminist Theology in a European Context* (1st Yearbook of the European Society of Women in Theological Research), eds. Annette Esser and Luise Schottroff (Kampen, Kok Pharos and Mainz, Matthias-Grünewald-Verlag, 1993), pp.11-37.
3. Julie Hopkins, 'Christologie oder Christolotrie? Einwände gegen die traditionellen Modelle von Jesus dem Christus' in *Vom Verlangen Nach Heilwerden: Christologie in feministisch-theologischer Sicht*, eds. Doris Strahm and Regula Strobel (Fribourg/Luzern, Edition Exodus, 1991), pp.37-51 and Julie Hopkins, 'Christology or Christolotry?' in *The Women's Movement: History and Theory*, eds. J.G.M.de Bruijn, L.D. Derksen and C.M.J.Hoeberichts (Aldershot, Avebury, Ashgate Publishing, 1993), pp.187-199.
4. Doris Strahm, 'Für wen haltet ihr mich? Einige historische und methodische Bemerkungen zu Grundfragen der Christologie' in *Vom Verlangen Nach Heilwerden*, pp.11-36.
5. Jon Sobrino, *Christology at the Crossroads* (London, SCM Press, 1978), pp.311-345.
6. Elizabeth Amoah and Mercy Amba Oduyoye, 'The Christ for African Women', in *With Passion and Compassion: Third World Women doing Theology*, eds. Virginia Fabella and Mercy Amba Oduyoye (Maryknoll, Orbis Books, 1989), p.44. See also, Mercy Amba Oduyoye, *Hearing and Knowing: Theological reflections on Christianity in Africa* (Maryknoll, Orbis Books, 1986).
7. Amoah/Oduyoye, 'The Christ for African Women', pp.35-46.
8. Chung Hyung Kyung, *Struggle to be the Sun Again* (Maryknoll, Orbis Books, 1990), pp.42-43, 64-71.
9. Gustavo Gutiérrez, *The Power of the Poor in History* (London: SCM Press, 1983),p.57.
10. Sharon Welch, *Communities of Resistance and Solidarity: A Feminist*

Theology of Liberation (Maryknoll, Orbis Books, 1985), p.72.

11. For a good introduction to the significance of post-modernist deconstructionism for contemporary theology see Sallie McFague, *Models of God* (London, SCM Press, 1987), pp.21-28.

12. The following pages are based upon a lecture I gave at the conference, 'Feministische Theologie und Christologie: Kritik und Neuansätze' held at the Evangelische Akademie Hofgeismar, Germany, 21st-23rd May, 1993.

13. Rosemary Radford Ruether, *New Woman New Earth: Sexist Ideologies and Human Liberation* (New York, Seabury Press, 1975), pp.20-23, 76-78.

14. The cases studies were conducted between 1991-1994 for the course 'Vrouwenpastoraat'in the Predikanten Opleiding, for the Faculteit der Godgeleerdheid, Vrije Universiteit, Amsterdam. The interviews were confidential and therefore remain unpublished.

15. This existential dilemma, which can lead to mental health problems, is powerfully analysed by the Dutch clinical psychologist and theologian Aleid Schilder in *Hulpeloos maar schuldig* (Kampen, Kok, 1987).

16. For a feminist critique of the Protestant teaching that sin is fundamentally pride and self-love see, Judith Plaskow, *Sex, Sin and Grace: Women's Experience and the Theologies of Reinhold Niebuhr and Paul Tillich* (London, University Press of America, 1980) and Joan Arnold Romero, 'The Protestant Principle: A Woman's Eye View of Barth and Tillich' in *Religion and Sexism*, ed. Rosemary Radford Ruether (New York, Simon and Schuster, 1974), pp.319-340.

17. The conference is mentioned in note 12.

Chapter 2 / Jesus: Object of Research and Focus of Faith

1. Jesus to the Samaritan woman according to John 4 v21.

2. A.Van Harvey, *The Historian and the Believer* (London: SCM Press, 1967), pp.280-281.

3. Elisabeth Schüssler Fiorenza, *In Memory of Her: A Feminist Theological Reconstruction of Christian Origins* (London: SCM Press, 1983).

4. Leonard Swidler, *Biblical Affirmations of Women* (Philadelphia, Westminster Press, 1979) and Elisabeth Moltmann-Wendel, *The Women Around Jesus* (London, SCM Press, 1982).

5. Exodus 20 v.12.

6. Judith Ochshorn, *The Female Experience and the Nature of the Divine*

(Bloomington, Indiana University Press, 1981), p.173.

7. Daphne Hampson and Rosemary Radford Ruether, 'Is There a Place for Feminists in a Christian Church?' *New Blackfriars* (January 1987), p.5.

8. John Hick, 'Problems of Religious Pluralism' in his, *A Philosophy of Religious Pluralism* (London, The MacMillan Press, 1985), pp.28-45.

9. Elisabeth Schüssler Fiorenza, 'The Function of Scripture in the Liberation Struggle: A Critical Feminist Hermeneutics and Liberation Theology' in her *Bread not Stone: The Challenge of Feminist Biblical Interpretation* (Boston, Beacon Press, 1984), p.60.

10. Roemary Radford Ruether, *To Change the World: Christology and Cultural Criticism* (London: SCM Press, 1981), p.3.

11. Albert Schweitzer, *The Quest of the Historical Jesus*(1906), trans.W.Montgomery (New York: The Macmillan Co.,1964).

12. Karl Barth, *Der Romerbrief* (2nd ed. Munich: Chr.Kaiser Verlag, 1921),(English ed. *The Epistle to the Romans*, Oxford: Oxford University Press, 1968).

13. John Macquarrie, *Twentieth Century Religious Thought: The Frontiers of Philosophy and Theology 1900-1980* (London: SCM Press, 1981), p.377.

14. Ibid., pp.377-379.

15. James M.Robinson, *The New Quest of the Historical Jesus* (London: SCM Press, 1959).

16. For a good review of the discussion about the nature of the gospel genre and its closest literary antecedents see, Howard C.Kee, *Community of the New Age* (London: SCM Press, 1977), pp.14-49.

17. Helmut Koester, *Ancient Christian Gospels: Their History and Development* (London: SCM Press, 1990), pp24-29.

18. The extant Nag Hammadi texts were collated by a team of scholars and edited by James M.Robinson as *The Nag Hammadi Library* (Netherlands: E.J.Brill). For a thought-provoking introduction into their religious and social content as perceived by a woman member of the team see Elaine Pagels, *The Gnostic Gospels* (London: Penguin, Pelican Books 1979).

19. Oscar Cullmann first proposed the concept of Heilsgeschichte in his book *Christ and Time* (1949), (Eng.ed. London: SCM Press, 1967). Rudolf Bultmann criticised the term for confusing myth and history in the article 'Heilsgeschichte und Geschichte' in *Theologische Literaturzeitung*, LXXXIII (1948), pp.659-66. This is translated and reprinted in *Existence and Faith* ed. Schubert M.Ogden (London: Hodder and Stoughton, 1961), pp.226-240.

20. C.H.Dodd, *The Parables of the Kingdom* (1935), reprinted (London: Collins, 1961) and *The Apostolic Preaching and its Development* (London:

Nisbet, 1938).

21. Oscar Cullmann, *Salvation in History* (Tübingen: J.C.B.Mohr, 1965), Eng.ed.(London: SCM Press, 1967), p.33.

22. Rosemary Radford Ruether, *Sexism and God-Talk: Towards a Feminist Theology* (London: SCM Press, 1983), pp.237-255.

23. Rosemary Radford Ruether, 'Jesus and the Revolutionaries: Political Theology and Biblical Hermeneutics' in her *To Change the World*, pp.7-18.

24. Luke 4 vv.16-21.

25. This is the thesis of Geza Vermes in his book, *Jesus the Jew* (London, Collins, 1973), pp.69-80.

26. Oscar Cullmann, *Jesus and the Revolutionaries* (New York: Harper and Row, 1970).

27. James M.Robinson, 'Jesus as Sophos and Sophia: Wisdom Tradition and the Gospels' and Elisabeth Schüssler Fiorenza, 'Wisdom Mythology and the Christological Hymns of the New Testament', in *Aspects of Wisdom in Judaism and Early Christianity*, ed. R.L.Wilken (Indiana: University of Notre Dame Press, 1975), pp.1-16 and 17-41.resp. See also, James D.G.Dunn, *Christology in the Making* (London: SCM Press, 1980), pp.209-10.

28. A.Van Harvey, *The Historian and the Believer*, pp.266-7.

29. Rosemary Radford Ruether, *To Change the World*, p.22.

30. For an excellent discussion of the nature of androcentric language in the New Testament see, Elisabeth Schüssler Fiorenza, *In Memory of Her*, pp.41-67.

Chapter 3 / The Jesus Movement and the Kingdom of God

1. Jesus to his disciples according to Mark 3 v.35.

2. Elisabeth Schüssler Fiorenza, *In Memory of Her: A Feminist Theological Reconstruction of Christian Origins* (London: SCM Press, 1983), pp.105-159.

3. Fiorenza, Ibid., pp.140-151.

4. Nicola Slee, 'Parables and Women's Experience' *The Modern Churchman* 26, no.2 (1984), pp.25-31.

5. See Gerd Theissen, 'Wanderradikalismus: Literatursoziologische Aspekte der Überlieferung von Worten Jesu im Urchristentum', *ZTK* 70, (1973), pp.245-71: English trans. in *Radical Religion 2*, nos.2 and 3, Berkley (1975), pp.84-93.

6. Howard Kee, *Community of the New Age: Studies in Mark's Gospel* (London: SCM Press, 1977), p.89 and 104.

7. The text of *Jesus Christ Superstar: A Rock Opera* by Andrew Lloyd Webber and Tim Rice is available with the records from MCA Records, EMI Records Ltd, Hayes, Middlesex, 1970.

8. James D.G.Dunn, *Jesus and the Spirit* (London: SCM Press, 1975), p43.

9. Howard Kee, *Community of the New Age*, pp.7-9.

10. Ibid., pp.100ff.

11. H.J.Holtzmann, *Die synoptischen Evangelien. Ihr Ursprung und ihr geschichtlicher Charakter* (Leipzig 1863). For a discussion of the priority of Mark see, W.G. Kümmel, *The New Testament: The History of the Investigation of its Problems* (London: SCM Press, 1973), pp151-155.

12. William Wrede, *Das Messiasgeheimnis in den Evangelien* (Göttingen 1901): English trans., *The Messianic Secret* (Cambridge: 1971).

13. Hans-Georg Gadamer, *Truth and Method* (New York: Continuum Press,1975).

14. Howard Kee, *Community of the New Age*, pp.64-76.

15. I am aware that according to the 2nd century presbyter tradition of Clement of Alexandria and Papias of Hierapolis, Mark was regarded as the founder of the church in Alexandria in Egypt. I accept Kee's position that the semitically influenced Koiné Greek of Mark's Gospel makes this claim highly unlikely. For a full discussion of this possibility see Birger A.Pearson, 'Earliest Christianity in Egypt: Some Observations' in *idem* and James E.Goehring, eds., *The Roots of Egyptian Christianity* (Studies in Antiquity and Christianity; Philadelphia: Fortress Press, 1986), pp.137-4

16. For Ghana see, Elizabeth Amoah and Mercy Amba Oduyoye, 'The Christ for African Women', in *With Passion and Compassion: Third World Women doing Theology*, ed. Virginia Fabella and Mercy Amba Oduyoye (Maryknoll: Orbis Books, 1989), pp.35-46. For Korea see, Chung Hyung Kyung, *Struggle to Be the Sun Again* (Maryknoll: Orbis Books, 1990). For Japan/U.S.A. see, Rita Nakashima Brock, *Journeys by Heart: A Christology of Erotic Power* (New York: Crossroad, 1988).

17. For a scholarly account of the 'political' dimension of shamanism see, I.M.Lewis, *Ecstatic Religion: A Study of Shamanism and Spirit Possession* (2nd edition) (London: Routledge, 1991).

18. Rita Nakashima Brock, *Journeys by Heart*, pp.80-81.

19. Ibid.,p.105.

20. Jesus' predictions of his death are to be found in Mark 8v.31;9v.31 and 10v.33. His resurrection promises are Mark 14v.27f., and 16v.7.

21. Howard Kee, *Community of the New Age*, p.174.
22. Isabel Carter Heyward, *The Redemption of God: A Theology of Mutual Relation* (London: University Press of America, 1982), p.58.
23. Ibid.,p.57.
24. Rita Nakashima Brock, *Journeys by Heart*, p.107.
25. Elisabeth Schüssler Fiorenza, *In Memory of Her*, p.322.
26. Ibid.,p.323.

Chapter 4 / The Cross of Powerlessness

1. I Peter 2 v.24.
2. I Peter 2 v.18- 3 v.6.
3. Anselm, *Cur Deus Homo?* tr.S.N.Deane in, *St.Anselm: Basic Writings* ed., C.Hartshorne (Illinois: La Salle, 2nd edn 1962),pp.191-302.
4. For a feminist theological discussion of the Latin, Greek and modern models of atonement see, Mary Grey, *Redeeming the Dream: Feminism, Redemption and Christian Tradition* (London, SCM Press, 1989),pp.109-125.
5. Ibid.,pp.112-113.
6. For a critique of Christian masochism and theological sadism see, Dorothee Soelle, *Suffering* (London, Darton, Longman and Todd, 1975),pp.9-32.
7. For an excellent discussion of the anxieties of Sixteenth Century Europeans as encapsulated in the life and teaching of Calvin see, William J.Bouwsma, *John Calvin: A Sixteenth Century Portrait* (Oxford, Oxford University Press: 1988).
8. Aleid Schilder, *Hulpeloos maar schuldig* (Netherlands, Kampen, Kok, 1987).
9. Jürgen Moltmann, *The Crucified God*, Eng.tran. (London, SCM Press, 1974),p.246.
10. Jürgen Moltmann, *Theology of Hope*, Eng.tran. (London, SCM Press, 1967),p.338.
11. Augustine, *De Civitate Dei* 13,3- 13,14. For the English translation by Philip Levine see St.Augustine, *The City of God Against the Pagans* (LCL, 1966). For a feminist theological discussion of Augustine's teaching on Original Sin see, Elaine Pagels, *Adam, Eve and the Serpent* (London: Penguin Books, 1990),pp98-150.
12. Tertullian, *De Cultu Feminarum* I,12, I,1418b-19a.
13. Sara Maitland, 'Passionate Prayer: Masochistic Images in Women's

Experience' in *Sex and God: Some Varieties of Women's Religious Experience*, ed.Linda Hurcombe (London, Routledge and Kegan Paul, 1987).p.126. An abridged translation of the hagiographical account is to be found in, F.W.Faber, *The Saints and Servants of God* (London, 1847),pp.27-45.

14. Sara Maitland, Ibid.,p.127.
15. Annie Imbens and Ineke Jonker, *Godsdienst en incest* (Netherlands, Amersfoort, 1985).
16. Unpublished paper by Auli van't Spijker for *bijvak Feminisme en Theologie* (Amsterdam: Vrije Universiteit, 1991).
17. Friedrich Nietzsche, *Twilight of the Gods/ The Anti-Christ* (London, Penguin Books, 1988), p156.
18. Elisabeth Schüssler Fiorenza, *In Memory of Her: A Feminist Theological Reconstruction of Christian Origins* (London, SCM Press, 1983), pp68-96, 160-204.
19. Rita Nakashima Brock, *Journeys by Heart: A Christology of Erotic Power* (New York, Crossroad, 1988), pp54-55.
20. Jacquelyn Grant, *White Women's Christ and Black Women's Jesus: Feminist Christology A Womanist Response* (Atlanta, Georgia, Scholars Press, 1989), p213. The prayer is part of a collection in Harold A.Carter, *The Prayer Tradition of Black People* (Valley Forge, Judson Press, 1976), p49.
21. J.F. Bethune-Baker, *An Introduction to the Early History of Christian Doctrine: To the Time of the Council of Chalcedon*, 8th ed. (London, Methuen, 1946).
22. See Henry Chadwick, *Early Christian Thought and the Classical Tradition: Studies in Justin, Clement and Origen* (Oxford, Clarendon Press, 1966)
23. Don Cupitt, 'The Christ of Christendom' in *The Myth of God Incarnate*, ed. John Hick (London, SCM Press, 1977), pp135-6.
24. Grace Jantzen, *God's World, God's Body* (London, Darton, Longman and Todd, 1984), pp.67-100.
25. I Corinthians 13 v.7-8a.
26. Cited by John Bouwsma in *John Calvin*, p42.
27. For a fine contemporary discussion of the relationship between the historical background of the Book of Revelation and the author's use of traditional and apocalyptic material see, John Court, *Myth and History in the Book of Revelation* (London, SPCK, 1979).
28. This atmosphere is vividly recreated by Umberto Eco in his novel, *The Name of the Rose* (London, Pan Books, Picador edition, 1984).

29. John 19 v.25.

Chapter 5 / The Resurrection and Herstory

1. See Fritjof Capra, *The Tao of Physics* (Boston: Shambhala Pub. New Science Library, 1983).
2. Daphne Hampson in public debate with Rosemary Radford Ruether, 'Is There a Place for Feminists in a Christian Church?' *New Blackfriars* (January 1987),pp.13-14. For a detailed analysis of the christological implications of this debate see my essay, 'Sind Christologie und Feminismus unvereinbar? Zur Debatte zwischen Daphne Hampson und Rosemary Radford Ruether' in *Vom Verlangen Nach Heilwerden: Christologie in feministisch-theologischer Sicht* eds. Doris Strahm and Regula Strobel (Switzerland Fribourg/Luzern Edition Exodus 1991),pp.194-207.
3. Ernst Troeltsch, *Die Absolutheit des Christentums* (Tübingen: J.C.B.Mohr, 1902). English edition translated by James Luther Adams as *The Absoluteness of Christianity* (London, John Knox Press, 1972). For a thorough discussion of the Twentieth Century theological debate upon the meaning of history see A.Van Harvey, *The Historian and the Believer* (London, SCM Press, 1967).
4. Walter Otto, cited by Rosemary Radford Ruether, in, *Disputed Questions on Being a Christian* (Nashville: Abingdon, 1982) p.26.
5. Peter Berger, *The Sacred Canopy: Elements of a Sociological Theory of Religion* (New York: Doubleday, 1967; London: Faber and Faber, 1969).
6. Sallie McFague, *Metaphorical Theology: Models of God in Religious Language* (London: SCM Press, 1983), pp.4-7.
7. See Werner Kelber, *The Oral and Written Gospel* (Philadelphia: Fortress Press, 1983) and Rita Nakashima Brock, *Journeys by Heart: A Christology of Erotic Power* (New York: Crossroad, 1988),pp.35-49.
8. Sallie McFague, *Models of God: Theology for an Ecological Nuclear Age* (London: SCM Press, 1987).
9. Ruether and Hampson, *Is There a Place?* p.15.
10. Luke's account of Saul's vision in in The Acts of the Apostles ch.9 v1-30. Paul's own account constitutes part of his claim to apostolic authority in his letters to the Corinthians, see I Cor.9 v1-2; II Cor.11-12.
11. Rosemary Radford Ruether, *To Change the World: Christology and Cultural Criticism* (London: SCM Press, 1981), p.28.
12. John Mbitu, *New Testament Eschatology in an African Background*

(London: Oxford University Press, 1971), pp.24-31.

13. Bernadette Brooten, 'Early Christian Women and their Cultural Context: Issues of Method in Historical Reconstruction,' in *Feminist Perspectives on Biblical Scholarship*, ed. Adela Yarbro Collins (Missoula: Scholars Press, 1985), pp.65-66.

14. Elisabeth Schüssler Fiorenza, *In Memory of Her: A Feminist Theological Reconstruction of Christian Origins* (London: SCM Press, 1983).

15. Elisabeth Schüssler Fiorenza, 'Women-Church: The Hermeneutical Center of Feminist Biblical Interpretation' in her *Bread Not Stone: The Challenge of Feminist Biblical Interpretation* (Boston: Beacon Press, 1984), pp.1-22.

16. For a full discussion of the cult of Mary Magdalene see Elisabeth Moltmann-Wendel, *The Women Around Jesus* (English translation London: SCM Press 1982), pp.61-91.

17. The *Inter Insigniores*, popularly known as *The Vatican Declaration Against the Ordination of Women to the Ministerial Priesthood*, was issued by the Congregation for the Doctrine of the Faith and approved by Pope Paul VI on 15th October 1976 (the Feast of St.Theresa of Avila!). For the full text see, *L'Osservatore Romano* February 3, 1977, pp.6-8.

18. Jean-Jacques von Allmen, as quoted by Kallistos Ware in the latter's essay, 'Man, Woman, and the Priesthood of Christ', in Peter Moore ed., *Man, Woman and Priesthood* (London: SPCK 1978), p.71.

19. I Corinthians 15 v1-8.

20. Galatians 1 v11-24.

21. 'The Gospel of Mary', in *The Nag Hammadi Library* 473 ed.James M. Robinson (Netherlands: E.J.Brill),18.1-12.

22. For a clear account of this development see, Don Cupitt, 'The Christ of Christendom,' in *The Myth of God Incarnate*, ed.,John Hick (London: SCM Press, 1977), pp.138-143.

23. Daphne Hampson, *Theology and Feminism* (Oxford: Blackwell 1990), p.64.

24 See Theo Witvliet, 'De Epistemologische Breuk' in *Een plaats onder de zon* (Netherlands Baarn: Ten Have 1984) and Doris Strahm, 'Für wen haltet ihr mich?' in *Vom Verlangen Nach Heilwerden*, pp.11-36.

25. Rosemary Radford Ruether, *Sexism and God-Talk* (London: SCM Press, 1983), pp.116-138.

26. Manuela Kalsky, 'Elkaar tot spreken horen,' in *De gewonde genezer*, eds., Manuela Kalsky and Theo Witvliet (Netherlands Baarn: Ten Have, 1991), pp.169-197.

27. Nelle Morton, *The Journey is Home* (Boston: Beacon Press, 1985),

28. Jon Sobrino, *Christology at the Crossroads* (English edition London: SCM Press 1978), pp.195-6. Sobrino borrowed the expression, 'the monstrous power of negation' from the dialectical philosopher Hegel.
29. Mary Daly, *Gyn/Ecology* (English edition London: The Women's Press, 1979), p.79f.
30. Rita Nakashima Brock, *Journeys by Heart*, pp.100-104.
31. D.H.Lawrence originally named the novella, *The Escaped Cock* (Paris: The Black Sun Press, 1929) but he changed the title to *The Man Who Died* for the first English edition (London: Martin Secher, 1931).
32. Susan Thistlethwaite, *Sex, Race and God* (New York: Crossroad, 1991), p.108.

Chapter 6 / The Incarnation and the Quest for Female Subjectivity

1. Mary's reaction to the visit of the shepherds and the message of the angels according to Luke 2 v.19.
2. For a detailed account of the development of Logos theology in the Second and Third centuries by Tertullian and Novatian in the West and Origen in the East and its role in the Nicean and Chalcedon formulas see, Jaroslav Pelikan, *The Christian Tradition: A History of the Development of Doctrine* 'Book 1: The Emergence of the Catholic Tradition (100-600)' (Chicago and London: The University of Chicago Press, 1975), pp.172-266.
3. C.K.Barrett, *The Gospel According to John* (London, S.P.C.K., 1975), p.127.
4. Ibid.,p.29.
5. Oscar Cullmann, *The Christology of the New Testament* (London, SCM Press, 1973), p.253.
6. C.K.Barrett, p.128.
7. Ibid., pp.31-2.
8. The Wisdom sayings of Jesus are found in the Synoptic Gospels. In Matthew Jesus is identified with Sophia-God. See Elisabeth Schüssler Fiorenza, *In Memory of Her: A Feminist Theological Reconstruction of Christian Origins* (London, SCM Press, 1983), pp.130-140. For her discussion of the influence of Wisdom speculation on christology in the writings of Paul see, 'Wisdom Mythology and the Christological Hymns of the New Testament' in R.Wilken ed., *Aspects of Wisdom in Judaism and Early Christianity* (Notre Dame, University of Notre Dame Press,

1975), pp17-42.

9. The three New Testament passages are John 1 v.1 and v.14, I John 1 v.1 and The Book of Revelation 19 v.13.

10. Rosemary Radford Ruether, *Sexism and God-Talk: Towards a Feminist Theology* (London, SCM Press, 1983), p.117.

11. Anne-Claire Mulder, 'Vrouw, lichaam, subjectiviteit en het 'imago Dei'' in *Mara* jaargang 7 nummer 1 (September 1993), pp.3-13.

12. Mary Daly, *Beyond God the Father: Towards a Philosophy of Women's Liberation* (first ed.1973), (London, The Women's Press, 1986), p.19.

13. Ibid., p.77.

14. Jaroslav Pelikan, *The Emergence of the Catholic Tradition*, p.267.

15. See the collection of essays, *The Myth of God Incarnate* ed.John Hick, (London, SCM Press, 1977).

16. Isabel Carter Heyward, *The Redemption of God: A Theology of Mutual Relation* (Washington, University Press of America, 1982), p.31.

17. Carter Heyward, 'Doing Feminist Liberation Christology. Moving Beyond 'Jesus of History' and 'Christ of Faith': A Methodological Inquiry' in her *Speaking of Christ: A Lesbian Feminist Voice* (New York, The Pilgrim Press, 1989), p.16.

18. Ibid., p.14.

19. Idid., p.20.

20. Ibid., p.20.

21. Ibid., pp.21-22.

22. For a discussion of Brock's use of Christa-community see Chapter 3, p.43 and 46.

23. Dennis Nineham, 'Some Reflections on the Present Position with Regard to the Jesus of History', in his *Historicity and Chronology in the New Testament* (London, S.P.C.K., 1965), pp.9-10.

24. Pelikan, *The Emergence of the Catholic Tradition*, p.206.

25. Frances Young, 'Two Roots or a Tangled Mass?' in *The Myth of God Incarnate*, pp88-89. Origen wrote *Contra Celsum* in about 248 C.E.. Young follows the Loeb Classical Library translation, she also uses Henry Chadwick's, *Contra Celsum*.

26. Young, p.88. Origen, *Contra Celsum*, op. cit., vii.9.

27. Young, p.88.

28. Young, p.89. Origen, *Contra Celsum*, i.37.

29. Rosemary Radford Ruether, *Womanguides: Readings Towards a Feminist Theology* (Boston, Beacon Press, 1985), p.224.

30. Ibid., p.109.

31. Elaine Pagels, *Adam, Eve and the Serpent* Chapter 6, 'The Nature of

Nature' (London, Penguin Books, 1990), pp.127-150.

32. Letty Russell, *Human Liberation in a Feminist Perspective- A Theology* (Philadelphia, Westminster Press, 1974), p.136.
33. Ibid., pp138-9.
34. Ruether, *Sexism and God-Talk*, pp.109-115, 134-138.
35. Fiorenza, *In Memory of Her*, pp.343-351.
36. Ruether, *Sexism and God-Talk*, p.111.
37. Ibid., p.111. Since writing this essay I have become aware that Anne-Claire Mulder has made a similar and more detailed critique of Ruether's anthropology in the light of sexuel difference in an unpublished paper at the Feminist Seminar of 'The Society for the Study of Theology' (Soesterburg: April 1991). A revised Dutch version appears in *Proeven van vrouwenstudies theologie deel 3*, see note 46.
38. Pelikan, *The Emergence of the Catholic Tradition*, pp,263-4.
39. Paul Tillich, *Systematic Theology Vol.3* (London, SCM Press, 1984), pp.293-4.
40. Simone De Beauvoir, *Le Deuxième Sexe* (1949) Eng.tran.,H.M.Parsley as *The Second Sex* (Harmondsworth, Penguin Modern Classics, 1986).
41. For an excellent account of the projects of Hélène Cixous, Julia Kristéva and Luce Irigaray see Claire Duchen, *Feminism in France* (London, Routledge and Kegan Paul, 1986), pp.82-102.
42. Jacques Derrida, *La carte postale: de Socrate* á Freud et au-delá (Paris, Aubier-Flammarion, 1980), Eng.tran.,A.Bass, *The Post Card: From Socrates to Freud and Beyond* (Chicago, University of Chicago Press, 1987). See also Michel Foucault, *L'Ordre du discours* (Paris, Gallimard, 1971) Eng.tran. as 'The Discourse on Language' in his *The Archaeology of Knowledge* (New York, Random House, 1972).
43. For a good discussion of Lacanian and Post-Lacanian feminist psychoanalysis see Rosi Braidotti, 'Radical Philosophies of Sexual Difference or 'I Think Therefore She Is'', in her *Patterns of Dissonance: A Study of Women in Contemporary Philosophy* (Cambridge, Polity Press, 1991), pp.209-273. See also, Teresa Brennan, *Between Feminism and Psychoanalysis* (London, Routledge, 1989).
44. Luce Irigaray, *Ce sexe qui n'en est pas un* (Paris, 1977) Eng.tran. *This Sex Which is Not One* (Ithica, Cornell University Press, 1985).
45. Luce Irigaray, *Ethique de la Différence Sexuelle* (Paris, 1984) and, 'Femmes divines' in her *Sexes et Parentés* (Paris, Editions de Minuit, 1987), pp.69-85. For her critique of Fiorenza's *In Memory of Her* for its lack of incarnational christology see, Luce Irigaray, 'Equal to Whom?' in *Differences Vol.1* Nummer 2 (1988), pp.61-76.

125

46. Anne-Claire Mulder, 'Vrouw, lichaam, subjectiviteit en het 'imago Dei'', pp.9-13. For other articles by Mulder on Irigaray and the incarnation/divinization of the female subject see "Imago Dei: de mens (m/v) of 'man' en 'vrouw' als beeld van God: Het meensbeeld van Rosemary Radford Ruether bekeken vanuit het denken van Luce Irigaray', in Freda Droës (ed.), *Proeven van vrouwenstudies theologie deel 3* (Zoetermeer, Meinema, 1993), pp.17-43 and 'Goddelijk worden' in Agnès Vincenot, Marion de Zanger, Heide Hinterthür and Anne-Claire Mulder, *Renaissance: drie teksten van Luce Irigaray vertaald en becommentarieerd* (Amsterdam, Perdu, 1990), pp.140-160.

Chapter 7 / Concluding Christological Reflections

1. Jesus in answer to a question from the Pharisees according to Luke 17 v.21.
2. Mary Grey and Jana Opocenska, 'Upheavals and Change in Eastern Europe and its Reflection in Feminist Theology: a Dialogue' in Annette Esser and Luise Schottroff (eds.), *Feminist Theology in a European Context* (1st Yearbook of the 'European Society of Women in Theological Research')) (Kampen, Kok/Pharos and Mainz, Matthias-Grünewald-Verlag, 1993), pp.78-79.
3. Ibid., p.79. The quotation is from Eric Hobsbawn, 1989: 'To the Victor the Spoils', *The Observer* (3.2.1990).
4. Emmanuel Levina, *Autrement qu etre ou au dela de l'esse* (La Haye, Nijhoff, 1974).
5. Annelies Van Heijst, *Verlangen naar de val: Zelfverlies en autonomie in hermeneutiek en ethiek* (Kampen, Kok, 1992), pp.202-244.
6. Rosi Braidotti, 'Sexual difference as a Nomadic Political Project', lecture to the 5th Conference of the 'European Society of Women in Theological Research', Louvain 16-20 August 1993, (Conference Records *ESWTR*/1993), pp.1-26.
7. Ibid.,p.16.
8. Dale Spender, *For the Record: The Making and Meaning of Feminist Knowledge* (London, The Women's Press, 1985), p.71.
9. Rosemary Radford Ruether, *Sexism and God-Talk* (London, SCM Press, 1983), p.12.
10. Mary Grey, *The Wisdom of Fools? Seeking Revelation for Today* (London, SPCK, 1993).
11. Ibid., p.62.

12. Ibid., pp.27-8.
13. Ibid., p.99.
14. For example, in an article entitled 'Jesus Christ, Plain and Simple', *Time Magazine* reviews three books which have been published in the United States in 1993. These are, John Dominic Crossan, *Jesus: A Revolutionary Biography* (San Francisco, Harper), Burton Mack, *The Lost Gospel* (San Francisco, Harper) and The Jesus Seminar, *The Five Gospels* (Macmillan). See *Time Magazine*, January 10, 1994, pp32-33.
15. Jean Calvin, *Institutes of the Christian Religion*, Book 2 Chapter XV.
16. Vraag 32, 'Waarom wordt gij een Christen genoemd?' in *De Belijdenisgeschriften van de Nederlandse Hervormde Kerk* (1966),p71.
17. H.Berkhof, *Christelijk Geloof* (Nijkerk, G.F.Callenbach, 4th edition, 1979), pp.302-3.
18. The 'Society for the Study of Theology' Annual Conference was held at Westminster College, Oxford, 11th-14th April 1994.
19. Christoph Schwöbel, 'Christology and Trinitarian Thought', a paper presented to the *SST* Annual Conference, (April 1994), p.13.
20. For example, in discussing Moltmann's conception of the 'history of God' within the Trinity, Isabel Carter Heyward has argued that, 'It is as if Moltmann wraps a mythological blanket around history.' See her book, *The Redemption of God: A Theology of Mutual Relation* (Washington, University Press of america, 1982), p.213.
21. The feminist psychologist, Jean Baker Miller has argued that whilst these characteristics of female gender have been socially constructed as a result of the restriction of women to the private sphere, women should positively integrate them as a means of psychological and political liberation. See her book, *Towards a New Psychology of Women* (Boston, Beacon Press, 1976), pp.22-27.
22. Rosemary Radford Reuther, 'Witches and Jews: The Demonic Alien in Christian Culture' in her book, *New Woman New Earth: Sexist Ideologies and Human Liberation* (New York, Seabury Press, 1975), pp.89-114.
23. For an excellent discussion of the implications of religious pluralism for christology see John Hick, 'Religious Pluralism and Absolute Claims' in his book, *Problems of Religious Pluralism* (London, Macmillan Press, 1985), pp.46-65.
24. Rosemary Radford Ruether, *Women-Church: Theology and Practice* (London, Harper and Row, 1985), p.63.
25. The English mystical tradition of contemplating God through 'unknowing' is beautifully described by an anonymous writer in the Fourteenth Century book, *The Cloud of Unknowing*. For a scholarly criticism of the text see,

Phyllis Hodgson, *The Cloud of Unknowing and the Book of Privy Counselling* (Early English Text Society orig. ser. 218 (1944, reprinted with additions 1958).

26. See Mary Daly, *Beyond God the Father: Towards a Philosophy of Women's Liberation (1973) with Original Reintroduction* (London, The Women's Press, 1986) and Daphne Hampson, *Theology and Feminism* (Oxford, Basil Blackwell, 1990).

27. Daphne Hampson in debate with Rosemary Radford Ruether at the Westminster Cathedral Hall, London, May 1986. For the text of the debate see, Rosemary Radford Ruether and Daphne Hampson, 'Is There a Place for Feminists in a Christian Church?', *New Blackfriars* (January 1987), pp.1-16.

GENERAL BIBLIOGRAPHY

Amoah, Elizabeth and Oduyoye, Mercy Amba, 'The Christ for African Women' in *With Passion and Compassion: Third World Women Doing Theology*, eds., Fabella, Virginia and Oduyoye, Mercy Amba, (Maryknoll, Orbis Books, 1989), pp35-46.

Anselm, 'Cur Deus Homo?' Eng.tran.by S.N.Deane in *St.Anselm: Basic Writings*, ed.,Hartshorne, Charles, (Illinois, La Salle, 2nd edn. 1962), pp.191-302.

Augustine, 'De Civitate Dei' Eng.tran.,by Philip Levine in *St.Augustine, The City of God Against the Pagans* (Loeb Classical Library, 1966).

Barrett, C.K., *The Gospel According to John* (London, SPCK, 1975).

Barth, Karl, *Der Romerbrief* (1921), Eng.ed., *The Epistle to the Romans* (Oxford, Oxford University Press, 1968).

Berger, Peter, *The Sacred Canopy: Elements of a Sociological Theory of Religion* (London, Faber and Faber, 1969).

Berkhof, H., *Christelijk Geloof* (Netherlands, Nijkerk, G.F.Callenbach, 4th ed.,1979).

Bethune-Baker, J.F., *An Introduction to the Early History of Christian Doctrine: To the Time of the Council of Chalcedon*, 8th ed.,(London, Methuen, 1946).

Bouwsma, William J., *John Calvin: A Sixteenth Century Portrait* (Oxford, Oxford University Press, 1988).

Bultmann, Rudolf, 'Heilsgeschichte und Geschichte' in *Theologische Literaturzeitung LXXXIII* (1948), pp.659-66. Eng.tran., Schubert M.Ogden, *Existence and Faith* (London, Hodder and Stoughton, 1961), pp.226-240.

Braidotti, Rosi, *Patterns of Dissonance: A Study of Women in Contemporary Philosophy* (Cambridge, Polity Press, 1991).

Braidotti, Rosi, 'Sexual Difference as a Nomadic Political Project'. Lecture to the 5th Conference of the 'European Society of Women in Theological Research', Louvain 16-20 August 1993 (Conference Records ESWTR/1993), pp.1-26.

Brennan, Teresa, *Between Feminism and Pyschoanalysis* (London, Routledge, 1989).

Brock, Rita Nakashima, *Journeys by Heart: A Christology of Erotic Power*

129

(New York, Crossroad, 1988).

Brooten, Bernadette, 'Early Christian Women and the Cultural Context: Issues of Method in Historical Reconstruction', in *Feminist Perspectives on Biblical Scholarship*, ed., Collins, Adela Yarbro, (Missoula, Scholars Press, 1985), pp.60-66.

Calvin, John, *Institutes of the Christian Religion* (3 vols.), Eng.trans., Henry Beveridge (Edinburgh, Calvin Translation Society, 1865).

Capra, Fritjof, *The Tao of Physics* (Boston, Shambhala Pub., New Science Library, 1983).

Chadwick, Henry, *Early Christian Thought and the Classical Tradition: Studies in Justin, Clement and Origen* (Oxford, Clarendon Press, 1966).

Cullmann, Oscar, *Christ and Time* (1949), (Eng.trans., London, SCM press, 1967).

Cullmann, Oscar, *Salvation in History* (1965), (Eng.trans., London, SCM Press, 1967).

Cullmann, Oscar, *Jesus and the Revolutionaries* (New York, Harper and Row, 1970).

Cullmann, Oscar, *The Christology of the New Testament* (London, SCM Press, 1973).

Cupitt, Don, 'The Christ of Christendom' in *The Myth of God Incarnate*, ed., Hick,J., (London, SCM Press, 1977), pp.138-143.

Daly, Mary, *Beyond God the Father: Towards a Philosophy of Women's Liberation* (1973), (London, The Women's Press, 1986).

Daly, Mary, *Gyn/Ecology* (London, The Women's Press, 1979).

De Beauvoir, Simone, *Le Deuxième Sexe* (1949), Eng.tran., H.M.Parsley, *The Second Sex* (Harmondsworth, Penguin Modern Classics, 1989).

Derrida, Jacques, *La carte postale: de Socrate á Freud et au-delá* (1980), Eng. tran., A.Bass, *The Post Card: From Socrates to Freud and Beyond* (Chicago, University of Chicago Press, 1987).

Dodd, C.H., *The Parables of the Kingdom* (1935), (London, Collins, 1961).

Dodd, C.H., *The Apostolic Preaching and its Development* (London, Nisbet, 1938).

Duchen, Claire, *Feminism in France* (London, Routledge and Kegan Paul, 1986).

Dunn, James, D.G., *Jesus and the Spirit* (London, SCM Press, 1975).

Dunn, James, D.G., *Christology in the Making* (London, SCM Press, 1980).

Eco, Umberto, *The Name of the Rose* (London, Pan Books, 1984).

Esser, Annette and Schottroff, Luise, (eds.), *Feminist Theology in a European Context* (Netherlands, Kampen, Kok/Pharos, 1993).

Fiorenza, Elisabeth Schüssler, 'Wisdom Mythology and the Christological

Hymns of the New Testament', in *Aspects of Wisdom in Judaism and Early Christianity*, ed., Wilkin, R.L., (Indiana, University of Notre Dame Presss, 1975), pp.17-41.

Fiorenza, Elisabeth Schüssler, *In Memory of Her: A Feminist Theological Reconstruction of Christian Origins* (London, SCM Press, 1983).

Fiorenza, Elisabeth Schüssler, *Bread Not Stone: The Challenge of Feminist Biblical Interpretation* (Boston, Beacon Press, 1984).

Foucault, Michel, *L'Ordre du discours* (1971), Eng.tran.,'The Discourse on Language' in his, *The Archaeology of Knowledge* (New York, Random House, 1972).

Gadamer, Hans-Georg, *Truth and Method* (New York, Continuum Press, 1975).

Grant, Jacquelyn, *White Women's Christ and Black Women's Jesus: Feminist Christology A Womanist Response* (Atlanta, Georgia, Scholars Press, 1989).

Grey, Mary, *Redeeming the Dream: Feminism, Redemption and Christian Tradition* (London, SCM Press, 1989).

Grey, Mary, *The Wisdom of Fools? Seeking Revelation Today* (London, SPCK, 1993).

Gutiérrez, Gustavo, *The Power of the Poor in History* (London, SCM Press, 1983).

Hampson, Daphne, and Ruether, Rosemary Radford, 'Is There a Place for Feminists in a Christian Church?' *New Blackfriars* (January 1987),pp.1-16.

Hampson, Daphne, *Theology and Feminism* (Oxford, Blackwell, 1990).

Heyward, Carter, *The Redemption of God: A Theology of Mutual Relation* (London, University Press of America, 1982).

Heyward, Carter, *Speaking of Christ: A Lesbian Feminist Voice* (New York, The Pilgrim Press, 1989).

Hick, John, *A Philosophy of Religious Pluralism* (London, The MacMillan Press, 1985).

Hodgson, Phyllis, *The Cloud of Unknowing and the Book of the Privy Counselling* (Early English Text Society (1944) reprinted with additions, 1958)

Hopkins, Julie M., 'Christology or Christolotry?' in *The Women's Movement: History and Theory* eds., De Bruijn, J.G.M., Derksen, L.D., and Hoeberichts, C.M.J., (Aldershot, Avebury, Ashgate Publishing, 1993), pp.187-199.

Imbens, Annie and Jonker, Ineke, *Godsdienst en incest* (Netherlands, Amersfoort, 1985).

Irigaray, Luce, *Ce sexe qui n'en est pas un* (1977), Eng.tran., *This Sex Which is Not One* (Ithica, Cornell University Press, 1985).

131

Irigaray, Luce, 'Equal to Whom?' *Differences* Vol.1/2 (1988), pp.61-76.

Jantzen, Grace, *God's World, God's Body* (London, Darton, Longman and Todd, 1984).

Kalsky, Manuela, 'Elkaar tot spreken horen' in *De gewonde genezer* eds., Kalsky, Manuela and Witvliet, Theo, (Netherlands, Baarn, Ten Have, 1991), pp.169-197.

Kee, Howard C., *Community of the New Age* (London, SCM Press, 1977).

Koester, Helmut, *Ancient Christian Gospels: The History and Development* (London, SCM Press, 1990).

Kümmel, W.G., *The New Testament: The History of the Investigation of its Problems* (London, SCM Press, 1973).

Kyung, Chung Hyung, *Struggle to be the Sun Again* (Maryknoll, Orbis Books, 1990).

Lawrence, D.H., *The Man Who Died* (London, Martin Secher, 1931).

Levinas, Emmanuel, *Autrement qu etre ou au delá de l'esse* (La Haye, Nijhoff, 1974).

Lewis, I.M., *Ecstatic Religion: A Study of Shamanism and Spirit Possession* (London, Routledge, 1991).

Macquarrie, John, *Twentieth Century Religious Thought: The Frontiers of Philosophy and Theology 1900-1980* (London, SCM Press, 1981).

Maitland, Sara, 'Passionate Prayer: Masochistic Images in Women's Experience' in *Sex and God: Some Varieties of Women's Religious Experience*, ed., Hurcombe, Linda, (London, Routledge and Kegan Paul, 1987), pp.125-140.

Mbitu, John, *New Testament Eschatology in an African Background* (London, Oxford University Press, 1971).

McFague, Sallie, *Metaphorical Theology: Models of God in Religious Language* (London, SCM Press, 1983).

McFague, Sallie, *Models of God: Theology for an Ecological Nuclear Age* (London, SCM Press, 1987).

Miller, Jean Baker, *Towards a New Psychology of Women* (Boston, Beacon Press, 1976).

Moltmann, Jürgen, *Theology of Hope* (Eng.tran., London, SCM Press, 1967).

Moltmann, Jürgen, *The Crucified God* (Eng.tran., London, SCM Press, 1974).

Moltmann-Wendel, Elisabeth, *The Women Around Jesus* (Eng.tran., London, SCM Press, 1982).

Moore, Peter, *Man, Woman, and the Priesthood* (London, SPCK, 1978).

Morton, Nelle, *The Journey is Home* (Boston, Beacon Press, 1985).

Mulder, Anne-Claire, "Imago Dei': de mens (m/v) of 'man' en 'vrouw' als beeld van God: Het mensbeeld van Rosemary Radford Ruether bekeken vanuit het denken van Luce Irigaray' in *Proeven van vrouwenstudies theologie III* ed., Droës, Freda, (Netherlands, Zoetermeer, Meinema, 1993), pp.17-43.

Nag Hammadi Library, ed., Robinson, James M., (Netherlands, E.J.Brill).

Nietzsche, Friedrich, *Twilight of the Gods/the Anti-Christ* (1888) (Eng.tran., London, Penguin Books, 1988).

Nineham, Dennis, *Historicity and Chronology in the New Testament* (London, SPCK, 1965).

Ochshorn, Judith, *The Female Experience and the Nature of the Divine* (Bloomington, Indiana University Press, 1981).

Oduyoye, Mercy Amba, *Hearing and Knowing: Theological Reflections on Christianity in Africa* (Maryknoll, Orbis Books, 1986).

Pagels, Elaine, *The Gnostic Gospels* (London, Penguin, Pelican Books, 1979).

Pagels, Elaine, *Adam, Eve and the Serpent* (London, Penguin Books, 1990).

Pearson, Birger A., 'Earliest Christianity in Egypt: Some Observations', in *The Roots of Egyptian Christianity*, eds., idem and Goehring, James E.,(Studies in Antiquity and Christianity: Philadelphia, Fortress Press, 1986), pp.137-45.

Pelikan, Jaroslav, *The Christian Tradition: A History of the Development of Doctrine* (Book 1 *The Emergence of the Catholic Tradition 100-600),* (London, The University of Chicago Press, 1975).

Plaskow, Judith, *Sex, Sin and Grace: Women's Experience and the Theologies of Reinhold Niebuhr and Paul Tillich* (London, University Press of America, 1980).

Robinson, James M., *The New Quest of the Historical Jesus* (London, SCM Press, 1959).

Romero, Joan Arnold, 'The Protestant Principle: A Woman's Eye View of Barth and Tillich', in *Religion and Sexism* ed., Ruether,Rosemary Radford (New York, Simon and Schuster, 1974), pp.319-340.

Ruether, Rosemary Radford, *New Women, New Earth: Sexist Ideologies and Human Liberation* (New York, Seabury Press, 1975).

Ruether, Rosemary Radford, *To Change the World: Christology and Cultural Criticism* (London, SCM Press, 1981).

Ruether, Rosemary Radford, *Disputed Questions on Being a Christian* (Nashville, Abingdon, 1982).

Ruether, Rosemary Radford, *Sexism and God-Talk: Towards a Feminist Theology* (London, SCM Press, 1983).

Ruether, Rosemary Radford, *Womanguides: Readings Towards a Feminist*

133

Theology (Boston, Beacon Press, 1985).

Ruether, Rosemary Radford, *Women-Church: Theology and Practice* (London, Haroer and Row, 1985).

Russell, Letty, *Human Liberation in a Feminist Perspective - A Theology* (Philadelphia, Westminister Press, 1974).

Schilder, Aleid, *Hulpeloos maar schuldig* (Netherlands, Kampen, Kok, 1987).

Schweitzer, Albert, *The Quest of the Historical Jesus* (1906), Eng.tran., W.Montgomery (New York, The Macmillan Co., 1964).

Slee, Nicola, 'Parables and Women's Experience' *The Modern Churchman* 26, no.2 (1984), pp.25-31.

Sobrino, Jon, *Christology at the Crossroads* (London, SCM Press, 1978).

Soelle, Dorothee, *Suffering* (London, Darton, Longman and Todd, 1975).

Spender, Dale, *For the Record: The Making and Meaning of Feminist Knowledge* (London, The Women's Press, 1985).

Strahm, Doris and Strobel, Regula (eds.), *Vom Verlangen Nach Heilwerden: Christologie in feministisch-theologischer Sicht* (Switzerland, Fribourg/Luzern, Edition Exodus, 1991).

Thistlethwaite, Susan, *Sex, Race and God* (New York, Crossroad, 1991).

Tillich, Paul, *Systematic Theology Vol.3* (London, SCM Press, 1984).

Troeltsch, Ernst, *Die Absolutheit des Christentums* (1902), Eng.trans., James Luther Adams, *The Absoluteness of Christianity* (London, John Knox Press, 1972).

Van Harvey, A., *The Historian and the Believer* (London, SCM Press, 1967).

Van Heijst, Annelies, *Verlangen naar de val: Zelfverlies en autonomie in hermeneutiek en ethiek* (Netherlands, Kampen, Kok, 1992).

Young, Frances, 'Two Roots or a Tangled Mass? in *The Myth of God Incarnate* ed., Hick, J., (London, SCM Press, 1977), pp.87-121.